Family and Multifamily Work with Psychosis

Family and Multifamily Work with Psychosis provides a practical step-by-step guide for professionals treating psychosis using family work.

The authors draw on over ten years of experience working with family and multifamily groups where there are members with a psychotic disturbance. They provide helpful guidance on vital issues, including setting up initial group meetings, crisis intervention plans, group structure, problem solving and communication in the group. Subjects covered include:

- The Stress–Vulnerability Model
- The group structure and framework
- Family work in early psychosis
- Working with families of people suffering from psychosis and substance misuse
- What the family can do to be of help and support

This accessible, jargon-free guide will be of great interest to anyone interested in investigating the potential for using family work to treat those with psychosis.

Gerd-Ragna Bloch Thorsen is a psychiatrist and teacher of psychotherapy. She is the coordinator of family work at Stavanger Psychiatric Hospital, Norway and Deputy President of the Norwegian Psychiatric Association.

Trond Grønnestad is a psychiatric nurse and leader of an educational project about mental health.

Anne Lise Øxnevad is a psychiatric nurse and leader of the psychoeducational multi-family group division at Stavanger Psychiatric Hospital, Norway.

Guest contributors: Bente Arntzen, Christine Barrowclough, Anne Fjell and Jan Olav Johannessen

Family and Multifamily Work with Psychosis

A Guide for Professionals

Gerd-Ragna Bloch Thorsen, Trond Grønnestad and Anne Lise Øxnevad

Routledge
Taylor & Francis Group

LONDON AND NEW YORK

First published in Norwegian 2000 by Stiftelsen Psykiatrisk
Opplysning, Norway

First published in the English language 2006 by Routledge
27 Church Road, Hove, East Sussex BN3 2FA

Simultaneously published in the USA and Canada 2006
by Routledge 270 Madison Ave, New York, NY 10016

*Routledge is an imprint of the Taylor & Francis Group, an informa
business*

Typeset in Times by RefineCatch Limited, Bungay, Suffolk
Printed and bound in Great Britain by TJ International Ltd, Padstow, Cornwall
Paperback cover design by Hybert Design

This publication has been produced with paper manufactured to
strict environmental standards and with pulp derived from
sustainable forests.

British Library Cataloguing in Publication Data
A catalogue record for this book is available from the British Library

Library of Congress Cataloging-in-Publication Data
Thorsen, Gerd-Ragna Bloch.
  Family and multi-family work with psychosis /Gerd-Ragna Bloch
Thorsen, Trond Grønnestad, Anne Lise Øxnevad.
      p. ; cm. (The International Society for the Psychological
Treatments of the Schizophrenias and other Psychoses book series)
  Rev. English ed. of: Familie-arbeid ved psykoser / Anne Lise
Øxnevad, Trond Grønnestad, Bente Arntzen. 2000.
  Includes bibliographical references and index.
  ISBN13: 978-1-58391-726-8 (hbk)
  ISBN10: 1-58391-726-8 (hbk)
  ISBN13: 978-1-58391-727-5 (pbk)
  ISBN10: 1-58391-727-6 (pbk)
  1. Psychoses—Treatment. 2. Schizophrenia—Treatment. 3. Family
psychotherapy. 4. Psychosis—Patients—Family relationships. I.
Grønnestad, Trond. II. Øxnevad, Anne Lise. III. Øxnevad, Anne Lise.
Familie-arbeid ved psykoser. IV. Title. V. Series: ISPS book series.
  [DNLM: 1. Pyschotic Disorders—therapy. 2. Family Therapy—methods.
WM 200 T521f 2006]
RC512.T56 2006
362.2'6—dc 22

2006024034

ISBN13: 978-1-58391-726-8 (hbk)   ISBN10: 1-58391-726-8 (hbk)
ISBN13: 978-1-58391-727-5 (pbk)   ISBN10: 1-58391-727-6 (pbk)

The ISPS book series

The ISPS (the International Society for the Psychological Treatments of the Schizophrenias and Other Psychoses) has a history stretching back some 50 years during which it has witnessed the relentless pursuit of biological explanations for psychosis. The tide is now turning again. There is a welcome international resurgence of interest in a range of psychological factors in psychosis that have considerable explanatory power and also distinct therapeutic possibilities. Governments, professional groups, users and carers are increasingly expecting interventions that involve talking and listening as well as skilled practitioners in the main psychotherapeutic modalities as important components of the care of the seriously mentally ill.

The ISPS is a global society. It is composed of an increasing number of groups of professionals organized at national, regional and more local levels around the world. The society has started a range of activities intended to support professionals, users and carers. Such persons recognize the potential humanitarian and therapeutic potential of skilled psychological understanding and therapy in the field of psychosis. Our members cover a wide spectrum of interests from psychodynamic, systemic, cognitive and arts therapies to the need-adaptive approaches and to therapeutic institutions. We are most interested in establishing meaningful dialogue with those practitioners and researchers who are more familiar with biological-based approaches. Our activities include regular international and national conferences, newsletters and email discussion groups in many countries across the world.

One of these activities is to facilitate the publication of quality books that cover the wide terrain which interests ISPS members and a large number of other mental health professionals and policymakers and implementers. We are delighted that Brunner-Routledge of the Taylor & Francis group has seen the importance and potential of such an endeavour and has agreed to publish an ISPS series of books.

We anticipate that some of the books will be controversial and will challenge certain aspects of current practice in some countries. Other books will promote ideas and authors well known in some countries but not familiar to others. Our overall aim is to encourage the dissemination of existing knowledge and ideas, promote healthy debate and encourage more research in a most important field whose secrets almost certainly do not all reside in the neurosciences.

For more information about the ISPS, email *isps@isps.org* or visit our website *www.isps.org*

Brian Martindale
ISPS Series Editor

International Society for the Psychological Treatments of the Schizophrenias and Other Psychoses Book Series
Series Editor: Brian Martindale

Titles in the series

Models of Madness: Psychological, Social and Biological Approaches to Schizophrenia
Edited by John Read, Loren R. Mosher & Richard P. Bentall

Psychoses: An Integrative Perspective
Johan Cullberg

Evolving Psychosis: Different Stages, Different Treatments
Edited by Jan Olav Johanessen, Brian V. Martindale & Johan Cullberg

Family and Multifamily Work with Psychosis
Gerd-Ragna Bloch Thorsen, Trond Grønnestad & Anne Lise Øxnevad

Contents

Acknowledgements

Many people have contributed to this book: some have shared their ideas, others have written chapters. In Norway, both in Stavanger and in Oslo, numerous individuals and inspiring groups of professional colleagues engaged in psychoeducational family work as well as hundreds of family members have been through the 2 year programme. This book is based on Bill McFarlane's approach, modified by the group's experience gained over the last 10 years. We would like to thank everyone who has shared with us their knowledge and experience.

Special thanks go to Vlad Babayants in Russia; and Philippa Martindale and Harold Heller in England both for the translation and for rendering the book suitable for an English-speaking audience.

About the authors

Bente Arntzen is a psychologist who has worked for many years in the youth department at the psychiatric hospital in Stavanger. She is currently working with drug addiction and psychiatry at *FA- bo* Rehabilitation Centre, Stavanger, Norway.

Christine Barrowclough has over 20 years' clinical and research experience in psychological treatment for psychosis, with a special interest in the carer's response to mental illnesses. She is a professor of clinical psychology and is currently working at the Academic Division of Clinical Psychology, School of Psychiatry and Behavioral Sciences, University of Manchester. She is a prolific author who has published widely in this field both alone and, more recently, in cooperation with her colleagues, describing the evaluation of specialists' approaches to working with people with psychosis and co-morbid substance abuse.

Gerd-Ragna Bloch Thorsen is a psychiatrist and teacher of psychotherapy. She is the founder of Psychiatric Information Foundation, PRO-PSY, publishing company and information centre and is the coordinator of family work at the psychiatric hospital, Stavanger, Norway. She has published several books and booklets on various aspects of psychiatry and is currently deputy president of the Norwegian Psychiatric Association.

Anne Fjell is a clinical sociologist. She is a specialist family work consultant in the early intervention project of the Psychiatric Clinic, Ullevel Hospital, Norway. She has edited books on psychosocial treatment of psychosis and leads the family work team at Lien Psychiatric Centre, Oslo, Norway.

Trond Grønnestad is a psychiatric nurse and has worked as coordinator of family work at the Stavanger Psychiatric Hospital for many years. He is currently working as the leader of a project on psychiatric education and information in the community in Sandnes, Norway.

Jan Olav Johannessen is chief physician at the Stavanger Psychiatric Hospital. He is President of the International Society for the Psychological Treatment of Schizophrenia and other Psychoses (ISPS) and the leader of the multi-centre 'Early Intervention in Psychosis' (TIPS) project. He has produced many publications on aspects of schizophrenia and early intervention.

Anne Lise Øxnevad is a psychiatric nurse and leader of the psychoeducational multifamily group division at the psychiatric hospital, Stavanger, Norway.

Figures and tables

Foreword

Multifamily group psychoeducation can be conceptualized as a support network centred on the family itself. The family is joined by a clinician who seeks to forge an alliance with the family – an agreement to work collaboratively in responding to the unique needs of the ill family member. The clinician is, in turn, supported by a supervisor who provides information and guidance to the clinician (and in some cases directly to the family). The clinician also works actively with providers of community-based clinical, rehabilitative and residential programming to ensure the continuity and uniformity of treatment. The family also gains support from the other families they meet and work with in the psychoeducational workshop and multiple family group setting.

The target population for the application of this approach are the families of newly admitted – although not necessarily first-time – patients diagnosed with schizophrenia, schizoaffective or other psychotic disorders.

Other individuals with chronic or severe mental illness also appear to benefit from this approach, although effectiveness studies with some of those populations have not been completed. Patients can be discharged to a variety of post-hospital settings including parental home, sheltered, supportive or independent housing. The assumption is that the family (broadly defined) offers some consistent and lasting contact – or plans to provide this in the future. To the extent that he or she is able, the patient participates in the sessions as a full family member following the educational phase of the intervention. The clinician strives to involve as many as possible of those family members who have close contact with the recovering patient. In some instances people other than 'family' are asked to participate (i.e. close neighbours, good family friends, case managers, etc.). Individuals with a history of drug and/or alcohol abuse secondary to schizophrenia are considered appropriate candidates for this treatment, although the intervention is often supplemented by more specialized substance abuse treatment or programmes.

We have developed specific ways of working with families as part of a long-term treatment model designed to promote increasingly sophisticated coping skills for handling the many difficult problems posed by mental illness in a family member. These problems include such common issues as participation in rehabilitation programmes, medication compliance, the use of illicit drugs, alcohol abuse, violence and the range of positive and negative symptoms presented by the patient. Using our model of family psychoeducation, we have been able to reduce the rate of relapse of these patients to below 40% of what would have been expected had they received more traditional forms of treatment. More recent research demonstrates that over 50% of those with severe mental illness have achieved open employment and a much improved quality of life, combined with reduced burdens and enhanced satisfactions in caretaking, for family members and others who provide support. The end result is that this approach is the most cost-effective psychosocial treatment for schizophrenia that has yet been developed.

William R. McFarlane, MD
Director, Center for Psychiatric Research Maine Medical Center
Portland, Maine, USA

Preface

Work with the family carers of people with serious psychiatric illness is supported by a strong evidence base from a considerable number of randomized controlled trials, conducted in Europe, America, China and Japan. Despite this, few families receive the professional help from which they and their ill relatives could benefit substantially. The group in Stavanger have made determined efforts over the last decade to integrate family work into their clinical service. They chose the model developed by Bill McFarlane of multifamily groups, the content of which overlaps considerably with the approaches of the other centres in the USA and UK, although the method of delivery is unique. However, the Stavanger group is flexible in its practice and works with individual families in their homes as well as running the multifamily groups.

The group has developed an efficient service by instituting a rigorous training course for the therapists and educating the local management so that they understand the clinical advantages of family work and the need for investment in training and flexibility of working hours. In England, Grainne Fadden has succeeded in establishing family work in her service by a similar approach to changing the managerial culture. This appears to be a prerequisite to introducing a service that can be maintained over time.

In this book, the key clinicians in the Stavanger service give a detailed account of their approach. It is written in simple language, free of jargon, making it accessible to anyone interested in reproducing this successful enterprise. The text is illustrated with examples from families who have participated and enlivened with verbatim quotes from family members, including users. Practical tips and helpful advice abound.

The family service is closely allied with the TIPS project, aimed at early detection and intervention for people with schizophrenia, and the book contains guidelines for the engagement of young people and their families at the onset of the illness. There is also a chapter by Christine Barrowclough, from the Manchester group, on the management of the combination of schizophrenia and substance abuse, which is of great value to clinicians wrestling with this difficult problem.

I visited the Stavanger group many years ago during one of their schizophrenia days meetings and was impressed with their enthusiasm and determination to actualize family work. This early promise has been fulfilled in an impressive and exciting way and this book chronicles their progress in a manner that should stimulate others to emulate their success.

Professor Julian Leff
Emeritus Professor, Institute of Psychiatry
Kings College, London

Chapter 1

Introduction to family work

Introduction
Gerd-Ragna Bloch Thorsen

Schizophrenia is one of the most serious of the mental illnesses and one that has a great impact on the life of both patient and the patient's family. It strikes mostly young people between the ages of 15 and 25, women and men equally and, although there is a higher incidence in rural areas and among certain groups of immigrants, this form of psychosis is found all over the world. There are multiple symptoms: hallucinations, thought disorder, delusions, social withdrawal and loss of many functions. While the precise cause of the illness is unknown, the prognosis is serious. We know, however, that there may be multifactorial causation, including significant biological, psychological and social components.

The treatment of schizophrenia has had a difficult history. Although there was considerable optimism and hope following the initial release of various antipsychotic medications, they did not provide a cure, but rather minimized the symptoms, mostly the active ones, such as hallucinations and hyperactivity. Their effect on social withdrawal, lack of initiative and delusions was even poorer. In addition, these medications tended to produce disturbing and harmful side effects. This situation has improved with the advent of a new generation of antipsychotic drugs, but there is still a long way to go.

Different forms of psychotherapy have been tried over the years. While some have proved ineffective, others have proved useful, especially in combination with other treatments.

Over the last three decades, although promising reports on the psychoeducational approach have been published, we have not been able to find any published study where this kind of treatment has been applied in a systematic manner to all patients who could benefit from it. This illustrates the challenges people suffering from schizophrenia and their families have to face. Very few are offered optimal treatment with proven methods and continuity of care.

We also know that patients often exhibit symptoms of the illness for months or even years before they receive treatment. The excessive duration of untreated psychosis (DUP) has been documented in many different studies.

When it comes to preventing relapse after recovery from psychosis, there are good reasons to believe that psychoeducational family work can be as effective as medication-based treatment, a situation that has been established for more than 30 years through reputable research (Pitschel-Walz *et al.* 2001). Despite this, it has often proved very difficult to introduce family work in a systematic manner to our psychotic patients.

In Stavanger, Norway, the significance of this work began to emerge in the 1980s. We wanted to educate ourselves in family work and invited acknowledged authorities, Professor Julian Leff among them, to teach us.

In 1988 we found the courage to arrange the first family meetings and 40 families attended the three evening courses. We also provided help to start a next of kin association and participated in their support groups when required. However, although it became clear that activities like the evening courses were very important in providing information and creating a more open atmosphere, they were far from adequate from a therapeutic point of view.

In 1994 the foundations of the early intervention project were laid in Rogaland, Norway. Rogaland Mental Hospital (RMH) began an investigation into the duration of untreated psychosis of its patients, prior to hospitalization and contact with health services. It became obvious that the duration of untreated psychosis was far too long – 114 weeks on average – and that treatment started too late (see Larsen and Johannessen 1996). In the wake of this investigation, a project was formed with the aim of both initiating treatment at an earlier stage of the illness and offering to patients what we believed to be the optimal treatment. Later, the project was split in two: Rogaland county did extensive publicity in an attempt to reach patients at an earlier stage of the illness. The Ullevål sector in the Oslo commune and Roskilde, Denmark, offered the same optimal treatment as the patients in Rogaland received except for the publicity element. In this way we hoped to establish any therapeutic benefits of earlier treatment.

Prior to launching the project, we gave consideration to the notion of 'optimal treatment' and formed our judgment on evidence-based findings. The four main elements were:

1   The patient should receive optimal antipsychotic treatment with neuroleptics.
2   The patient should receive psychotherapeutic treatment from an experienced therapist.
3   The patients should be hospitalized when required, *within an appropriate therapeutic environment.*
4   The patient should be offered the psychoeducational family approach.

In order to achieve this, the following four decisions were undertaken:

1   We debated what should be considered 'the optimal antipsychotic medication'.
2   An extensive educational programme for psychotherapy of the psychoses was launched.
3   The hospital developed a long-term strategy with the aim of producing a therapeutic environment within the wards.
4   Professionals were to gain experience in psychoeducative family treatment.

Long before the project started, an open invitation had been sent to all the RMH staff to elicit interest in developing and conducting family work. A group of 15–20 professionals including doctors, psychologists, sociologists and nurses, met regularly to review the literature on the subject. We knew from previous experience that a patient's relatives appreciated meeting other relatives and exchanging experiences with them. We, therefore, felt it was natural to start multifamily groups. We spent considerable time discussing whether the patient should participate in the group. It became clear that these efforts would be insignificant if the patient did *not* participate in the entire process. Thus, it was decided that patients should be part of the groups. Thomas McGlashan of Yale, the senior researcher involved in the project, put us in contact with William McFarlane who had already developed a model for multifamily groups and had experience in running them. We chose to use his model. Since psychoeducational family work was part of the research protocol, we agreed to conform to this model throughout the project.

Having chosen the method and read the manual, we invited McFarlane to Norway for a weekend seminar to teach us how to conduct work in multi-family groups. Those who wanted to become group leaders used role play to prepare for about 1 year before pilot groups were started. These groups comprised patients and families; the patients were already known to us and had been ill for a couple of years. It was agreed that the groups in the pilot phase should run for 9 months, while the research project had a timeframe of 2 years.

During the preparatory work emphasis was placed on encouraging skilled specialists, with the right characteristics, to join the work; thus it was an enthusiastic and engaged group that started out. Two leaders in each group were to co-run the group fortnightly for several months. We arranged regular meetings with group leaders from Rogaland, Oslo and Denmark. McFarlane was invited to make yearly contributions. As our group leaders became more experienced, the meetings with McFarlane became an arena for the exchange of experience rather than a place for education.

As the work developed and more groups formed, it became obvious that we needed regular recruitment and education of new group leaders with a common system of preparation. This led to the formation of the 'Family TIPS Schools' in Stavanger and Oslo. Under this model, participants receive a theoretical education (2 weeks) and observe an existing family group. To qualify as a group leader, it is necessary to have run a group under the guidance of an experienced group leader. An institute for multifamily group leaders, with the purpose of stimulating this type of family work, was also started. At the same time, it was recognized that the quality of the work needed to be monitored.

Research by McFarlane *et al.* (1995) has made it clear that the treatment results depend on whether or not the protocol is followed and whether the method chosen is used as intended.

Now that we know how valuable and effective family work is (Falloon *et al.* 1984; Leff 1994; McFarlane *et al.* 1995), there is another challenge for us: to ensure that patients and their families have such opportunities themselves to engage in it. There is a challenge in retaining group leaders after the first exciting phase of innovation has passed. There is a challenge in recruiting new group leaders, and in maintaining the quality of the work performed. The feedback from the families and patients is, in this respect, a source of inspiration. However, it is the institution leaders' responsibility to ensure that family work is as uncomplicated as possible. It requires the provision of flexible working hours, some finances for administration and distribution, photocopying, materials and suitable refreshments. There should be a place for group leaders to meet regularly to discuss further development of the work and to share their experiences. This method can be used both in multifamily and single groups. The principles and methods of this work can be applied to different categories of patient and research on this is in continuous progress.

We believe that this method of family work has a clear place in everyday clinical work. Since its launch in 1997 more than 200 families have joined the programme in Rogaland and Oslo. The dropout rate is very low and is mainly due to practical problems. The participant satisfaction is very high and, as the results of the research become apparent, it will be exciting to see if they reflect and confirm our clinical observations.

Background to family work
Trond Grønnestad

Psychiatry has always been characterized by a kind of mystique. Someone suffering from mental illness was perceived to change character and become a different person. In the Middle Ages many mentally ill people were burnt as witches and, even today, some religious communities claim that psychotic patients are in the grip of evil spirits. Despair and resignation were characteristic of psychiatric institutions. Neither cause nor remedy of the disease was understood. The history of psychiatry makes for painful reading. Given the lack of effective methods, treatments were applied that we might now consider torture, raising questions about the compassion of such carers.

Until the 1950s there was no efficient medication for psychotic symptoms. Staff carried out their duties diligently, believing in the validity of their approach. When antipsychotic medicines were introduced in the mid-1950s it was believed that the right treatment for the psychoses had finally been found. For the first time it became possible to treat patients with psychotic symptoms using medication that was effective. Treatment optimism in the western world was growing. In the wake of the discharge of psychiatric long-term patients, wide-scale closures of large psychiatric institutions were set in train. This meant that the important task of maintaining care for the patient was devolved to the family. Today, one-third of all patients with chronic mental illnesses live permanently at home with their families:

> Thus the role of the family has changed from being visitors *to* the long-term institutions to becoming the main caregivers for the person with long-term psychotic condition living at home.
>
> (Smeby in Hummelvoll and Lindstrem 1997)

This change was introduced without providing the local community or the family with the resources necessary to discharge these new responsibilities. Without such contributions from patients' families the closure of the largest institutions would not have been possible. Paradoxically, at the same time as discharging patients back to their homes, many specialists believed it was the patient's relatives who had caused mental illness, such as schizophrenia:

> Recent researches into the family prove that the family itself *cannot* be the only reason for a person's developing a serious mental disorder. The earlier belief that the patient's family was the prime cause of the illness underlay the negative attitude towards the patient's relatives that prevailed in Psychiatry. Instead of being given knowledge and strategies *for* handling the new situation they were ignored and misunderstood.
>
> (Smeby in Hummelvoll and Lindstrem 1997)

In order to be able to help a suffering family, those of us who work in the area of mental healthcare need to understand the causal links. If we rely on theories stating that the family negatively affects the patient, then our chances of helping that family are poor. Just as we condemn the way our earlier colleagues treated patients, our successors may condemn the way we treat patients' families. And just as our earlier colleagues believed their treatment methods were correct, we too believed that our attitude towards patients' relatives was right because of our theories that the family caused the illness.

Frieda From-Reichmann's term the 'schizophrenogenic mother' is familiar to many (Haugsgjerd 1990). This describes a cold, dominant and conflict-causing personality who brings schizophrenia upon her offspring. Of course, cold and conflict-causing people – those who send out double messages (Bateson 1972) – and families where communication between the members is contradictory, incoherent and confusing (Lidz and Fleck 1985), do exist. But there is no compelling evidence that these factors themselves cause the illness. Moreover, there appears to be no connection between these factors and the development of schizophrenia. What has become clear, however, is that during the last 30 years these theories have influenced our opinion about families and this has proved an obstacle to collaboration.

Expressed emotion

In the early 1960s the English psychiatrist George Brown and his co-workers carried out research into factors that contributed to a better or worse prognosis of relapse in patients suffering from schizophrenia (Leff and Vaughn 1985).

They investigated family and environmental factors in order to see what influenced the relapse rate in patients with schizophrenia. The trigger for this was the fact that those patients who, after hospitalization, returned to their homes and stayed with close relatives relapsed more often than those who were discharged from hospital to some other setting. Out of 600 different variables, these researchers identified three that influenced relapse and two that contributed to recovery. The variables that were deemed decisive for relapse were *critical comments towards the patient, hostility towards the patient* and *emotional over-involvement (EOI)*. Variables found to minimize relapse were *warmth* and *positive comments towards the patient*:

- **Critical comments** are rejecting remarks, words expressing dislike, contradiction, bitterness, resentment, etc. or remarks made in a critical voice.
- **Hostility** is considered to be present where it is perceived intensely by the patient or where global criticism is directed towards the patient.
- **Emotional over-involvement** refers to self-sacrifice, overprotection or over-identification with the patient.

To be able to measure these variables, the team developed a semi-structured interview – the Camberwell Family Interview (CFI) – which takes 1½ hours and is recorded onto a video- or audiotape, and then scored (Borchgrevink *et al.* 1999; Kavanagh 1992; Leff and Vaughn 1985).

Close family members of someone suffering from schizophrenia are interviewed about their feelings for or attitudes towards the patient. If one of the near relatives scores high on criticism, hostility or emotional over-involvement, then the family is rated a *high EE family*. If they score low on all the three variables they are held to be a *low EE family*.

In 1972 Brown and his co-workers carried out the first study based on the Camberwell Family Interview, to determine the difference between relapse frequency in low and high EE families (Leff and Vaughn 1985). They discovered that 58% of the patients discharged to high EE families suffered a relapse after 9 months, while in low EE families the figure was 16%.

Expressed emotions (EE) is a concept used to describe the feelings and attitudes expressed by a relative towards the patient during the Camberwell Interview. Later it was developed into a less time-consuming method for measuring EE – the Five-Minute Speech Sample (FMSS) (Mangana *et al.* 1986). Here family members, after a short introduction, talk about the ill member for 5 minutes. The Five-Minute Speech Sample scores criticism and over-involvement. Hostility is not scored in this interview.

Compared to the Camberwell Interview, the Five-Minute Speech Sample underscores criticism; nevertheless, it is a very good instrument for scoring expressed emotions.

Research on expressed emotions

In 1976 Julian Leff conducted a study of patients suffering from schizophrenia who were in the care of their families. The research showed a tendency to relapse after 9 months (Vaughn and Leff 1976). The experiment showed that feelings expressed in the family had an impact on the relapse rate. Yet, this finding tells us little about the cause of the illness.

It is important to stress that the level of EE is not a measurement of how good or bad a family is, but how they cope with the burden of having a member with a psychiatric illness. If the family is struggling with the consequences of the illness, then tensions within the family will be higher. A family with a high level of tension can be less burdened than that with a low level of tension before the patient relapses. However, it is also important to remember:

- EE varies over time, probably because of life events
- EE also characterise the patient's sufferings, and not only the family's
- Reduced EE is not necessarily the most important element in a successful family intervention
- Low EE is not always a sign of a well-functioning family
- Low EE families need help, too

(Hughes and Yeoman 1995)

The concept of expressed emotion has helped clinicians and researchers understand more of what is useful in the treatment of patients with psychosis. The concept has served as a basis for different forms of psychoeducational family intervention where the goal is to lower EE through education, communication skills training and active support for the family.

What does expressed emotion mean to families and to the individual patient?

As mentioned earlier, EE is measured through a structured interview – the Camberwell Interview or the Five-Minute Speech Sample. The concept is that the substance of what a near relative says about the patient is very similar to what that relative would actually say when speaking with or to the patient. This means that dissatisfaction, critical comments, etc. expressed in the interview will also show in their communication with the patient. Our thoughts influence our feelings which, again, are revealed through our attitudes and behaviour.

Table 1.1 demonstrates how that can occur in a family situation (see Borchgrevink *et al.* 1999).

What does high EE mean to the clinician?

The clinician should bear in mind that EE will or can vary together with the patient's condition and other psychosocial stress factors related to the family. Even then EE can tell the clinician something about what the family is struggling with and how this comes to show in relationship between the family and the patient.

Critical remarks made about the patient can be explained by lack of understanding of the consequences of the illness; negative symptoms related to psychosis can easily be taken for laziness; criticism towards the patient can also be caused by the stress and unhappiness experienced by relatives.

In such situations, the clinician may recognize a family that is in need of education, support and help to work through the crisis.

In the same way, over-involvement can be viewed as a process whereby the relatives gradually compensate for the patient's lack of self-care and finally find themselves in a condition they cannot tolerate. For the family to break this 'deadlock' it is necessary to let them know that others will take up the responsibility for the patient; they need to be reassured that their ill son or

Table 1.1 Attitude in relation to expressed emotion

Attitude	Low EE Relations	High EE Relations
Cognitive	Illness Fewer expectations	Doubtful about the illness/ laziness Higher expectations
Emotional	Focused on others Calm Objective	Self-focused High expression of anger Intense expression of distaste
Behaviour towards the patient	Adaptable Flexible Problem solving Non-intrusive Non-confrontational Indifferent	Less flexible Intrusive Confronting Overprotective

daughter will not suffer if others take over part of their duties in relation to the patient.

Psychoeducational family intervention

The EE research has proved to be almost directly transferable to clinical work and forms the basis for many different psychoeducational approaches. The breakthrough in psychoeducational family intervention occurred in 1978, when Michael Goldstein published the first results of a controlled study where the psychoeducational approach had been used (Goldstein *et al.* 1978).

A number of later studies explicitly documented the use of treatment approaches that regarded the family as part of the treatment team and supported the family's belief that they could be of help to the ill family member. The best known studies are as follows. (Falloon 1982, Leff 1985 and McFarlane 1990 can all be found in Borchgrevink *et al.* 1999.)

Ian Falloon, 1982

Falloon's study was based on single-family groups including the patient, where the treatment consisted of education, problem solving and communication training (Falloon *et al.* 1984). The model was designed with a special emphasis on communication training. The meetings were mostly conducted in the patient's home. The programme consisted of 40 meetings over 2 years. At the beginning there were weekly meetings then, gradually, they were held less frequently. In this study, the relapse rate after 9 months was only 6%, while the control group that received individual standard treatment had a relapse rate of 44%.

Julian Leff, 1985

Leff's study was based on single-family groups with or without the patient (Leff and Vaughn 1985). The meetings were held at the patient's home every 14th day over a period of 9 months. It was not as structured as Falloon's groups. The treatment consisted of education, communication training and problem solving. The relapse rate after 9 months was 8%.

Hogarty et al. 1986

This was a comparative study of four different treatments (Hogarty *et al.* 1986). All the patients participating in the study received optimal medication. In the groups with traditional treatment, the relapse rate after one year was 49%. In the psychoeducational single-family group the rate was 19% and the social skills training group it was 20%. When both social skills training and psychoeducational family intervention groups were offered the relapse rate after one year was 0%.

William McFarlane, 1990

McFarlane studied psychoeducational multifamily groups (five families in a group) (McFarlane 1990). The patients participated in the group. The treatment consisted of education, communicative skills training and problem solving. The families met every 14th day for 2 years.

McFarlane compared multifamily groups to single-family groups and dynamic-oriented multifamily groups. In the multifamily groups, the relapse rate after 1 year was 12%, in the single-family groups it was 29%, while the dynamic-oriented multifamily groups had a relapse rate of 42.9%.

Increased strain

The relationship between the person with a mental illness and the rest of the family will show a strong mutuality. Just as various aspects of the patient's home environment – for instance, emotional climate and social support – affect the course of the mental illness, the family, in its turn, may experience severe strain in its attempt to cope with the illness. The term 'strain' has much in common with the term 'social coping'. One person's poor coping is another person's strain. Strain is proportional to social expectations, which are likely to vary across families.

In 1966 Brown and colleagues described how the illness of one of the family members affected the rest of the family (Brown *et al.* 1966). They found that the patient's relatives often experienced severe and lasting stress which could test the boundary of what is normally regarded as acceptable. In periods of acute impairment of the patient's condition, the families had to weigh the impact of maintaining the patient at home with that of the patient's readmission to hospital.

What underlies this pattern of response? Factors at work include the general stigma attached to serious mental illness; disregard by health services of the needs of the patient's relatives; and the sense of blame attaching to families for their perceived negative impact on the patient. All this suffering leads to a chronic and downhill process. The characteristics of mental illnesses can explain why this suffering is special and progressive.

The term used by Smeby *et al.* (1998), 'empathic suffering', well illustrates the kind of suffering felt in identification with a person in pain. The family of someone suffering from schizophrenia must witness their close relative undergoing a painful process. They observe the sick person losing their sense of reality, changing their mode of communication and becoming psychotic. This is 'empathic suffering' – you feel another person's pain, you suffer with the rest of the family, you suffer because of your own loss of your son, daughter, mother, father, sibling, wife or husband. The psychotic person as well as the family may lose the social expectations related to each specific role and the relationship may change in significant ways. This reciprocal loss has not been widely described in the literature, but it is easily perceived from our own understanding of family process. There is, in addition, pain over what has been lost as well as pain over what will not now happen; that is, the loss of a future that had been anticipated.

The family must endure the patient's illness from adolescence through adulthood and must face the final anxiety about the care of their son or daughter when they have died.

To sum up, when a family member has a serious psychiatric disorder, it is not only the patient who suffers but the entire family. If we do not see the family's pain and its right to get support for itself, then it is not just the family that we let down, but the patient as well. The family is often the patient's most important resource. If it does not receive appropriate help then it may become overwhelmed in its task of supporting the patient. If we fail to help the family we deny the patient access to this important source of support.

Work with relatives requires the capacity to 'step into their shoes' and catch a glimpse of their pain.

In *Schizophrenia and the Family* (Anderson *et al.* 1986), a mother says about one of the staff: 'She was very nice, but I could tell from the way she asked questions that she was trying to find out what I had done wrong.' The mother went home and had a sleepless and tearful night, wondering what she had done that might have caused her son's schizophrenia. This story is not unique. Indeed, it happens every day.

The purpose of this book is to provide an insight into a new way of relating to the patient's relatives. We do not deal in questions of guilt and causation. We do indeed have theories and data that can tell us something about why some people may develop schizophrenia, but nobody can say why this John or that Mary has become ill. Nobody knows the patient better than his or her closest relatives and nobody is willing to sacrifice as much to help the patient as they are. If we can link this with our knowledge of psychiatric disorders then the patient's chances of recovery increase considerably.

The stress/vulnerability model
Trond Grønnestad

The theoretical model for serious mental illnesses that is used as an explanatory framework for psychoeducational family intervention is usually the stress/vulnerability model (Bentsen 1999). This model explains the onset of the disease, its course and social functioning as a complex interaction between biological, environmental, and behavioural factors (see Figure 1.1).

According to this model the symptoms of, for instance, schizophrenia, are the consequence of psychobiological vulnerability combined with environmental stress. In 1977 Zubin and Spring were already observing:

There are two major components of vulnerability, the inborn and the acquired. We have described inborn vulnerability as that which is laid down in the genes. The acquired component of vulnerability is due to the influence of traumas, specific diseases, peri-natal complications, family experiences, adolescent peer interactions, and other life events that either enhance or inhibit the development of the subsequent disorder.

(Zubin and Spring 1977: 109)

This psychobiological vulnerability makes the patient less able to handle the type of stress that comes with normal development. This explains why some

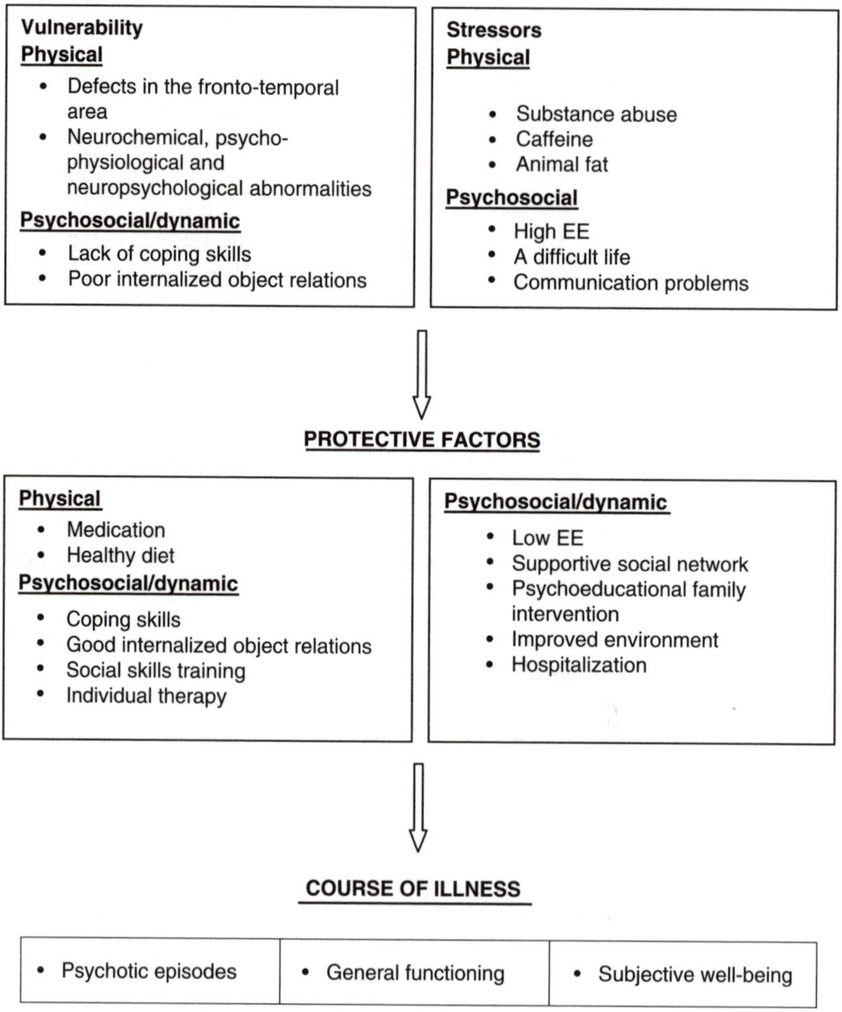

Vulnerability
Physical
- Defects in the fronto-temporal area
- Neurochemical, psycho-physiological and neuropsychological abnormalities

Psychosocial/dynamic
- Lack of coping skills
- Poor internalized object relations

Stressors
Physical
- Substance abuse
- Caffeine
- Animal fat

Psychosocial
- High EE
- A difficult life
- Communication problems

PROTECTIVE FACTORS

Physical
- Medication
- Healthy diet

Psychosocial/dynamic
- Coping skills
- Good internalized object relations
- Social skills training
- Individual therapy

Psychosocial/dynamic
- Low EE
- Supportive social network
- Psychoeducational family intervention
- Improved environment
- Hospitalization

COURSE OF ILLNESS

| • Psychotic episodes | • General functioning | • Subjective well-being |

Figure 1.1 The stress/vulnerability model (Bentsen 1999).

but not all children in the same family become ill. It can also explain why, in some families, cases of mental illnesses are quite frequent. This psycho-biological vulnerability is mainly due to genetic and developmental factors, while behaviour such as substance abuse can increase this vulnerability (Liberman 1989). When people with psychobiological vulnerability experience stress in their environment, they may undergo psychotic breakdown.

The development of schizophrenia is, as described earlier, a process that takes many years, but it is considered that the onset of the illness happens when the patient's stress tolerance has been exceeded (see Figure 1.2).

In this regard, stress and stressors are factors adding to disturbance. Stressors can be divided into two main categories:

Physical stressors:
- alcohol and drugs
- caffeine.

Psychosocial stressors:
- high expressed emotions (high EE)
- a difficult life
- communication problems.

What is experienced as a stress factor will vary from person to person, depending on individual competencies. For example, for someone with the relevant resources, it is not a stressful event to take a bus. Stress is often connected to the ability to adjust to particular situations. Day-to-day stresses seem to have a more profound impact in relation to the onset of psychotic episodes. It is understandable that the experience of stress may be more marked in early adulthood, when the illness has just started. Stress arising

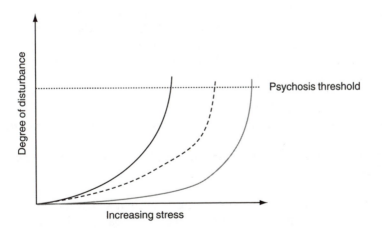

Figure 1.2 Stress tolerance in different people.

from academic studies or moving away from home, from a first job, or unemployment, from developing close relationships or becoming independent – all these may be experienced by young people as stressful. If there is also an underlying vulnerability or predisposition present, this can be enough to trigger the illness. If we exclude psychoses caused by drug use or brain damage, we can assume that there is always an element of stress as a context for the development of psychosis. More stressful events such as, for instance, the death of a relative, loss of work or the breakup of a relationship seem to intensify the psychotic symptoms or may actually trigger a new psychotic episode.

Robert P. Liberman introduced the term 'vulnerability and stress and competence model'. He uses the terms 'vulnerability' and 'stress' as described earlier, but introduces the notions of 'protection factors' and 'competence'. *Competence* is directly linked to *vulnerability*. Competence is a set of abilities and skills we have within us. As a person gains greater competence, he is able to deal with a greater amount of stress before becoming disturbed. Therefore, the development of competence will be a protective factor that directly reduces vulnerability (Liberman 1989). *Protective factors* are those aspects that minimize vulnerability and reduce psychosocial stress. We can divide protective factors into three main categories:

- **Medication** that reduces vulnerability.
- **Full social support**, including withdrawal (where required), milieu therapy, coordination of welfare services with the resources of family and friends.
- **Skills training**. This protective factor directly influences vulnerability and covers training in skills that would, for example, allow the patient to use a bus; ADL (activity of daily living) skills, i.e. daily hygiene, washing, eating, etc.; and social behavioural training, such as symptom management, communication skills etc.

The stress/vulnerability model can help us understand why a person has become ill, but it is, primarily, a means of finding out which methods of treatment might prove effective and which might not.

The model is also an excellent tool for investigating what has gone wrong in cases of relapse. For example:

Did he stop taking his medication?
Has he been exposed to major stress or has there been a change in the social support system?
Perhaps he has had less contact with the family or was dismissed from his job etc.

This framework makes it possible to find out, in a systematic way, what has changed and to make corresponding efforts to balance the scales (see Figure 1.3).

Good adjustment

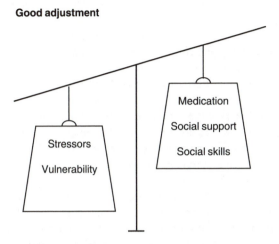

- Reduced symptoms
- Contact with others
- Independent living
- Stable work/business or education

Moderate adjustment

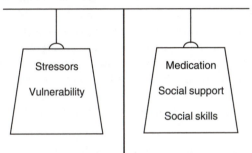

- Stable symptoms
- Regular medication
- Day centre
- Sheltered employment

Poor adjustment

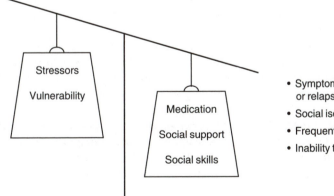

- Symptoms worsening or relapse
- Social isolation
- Frequent hospitalization
- Inability to work

Figure 1.3 Balancing the scales of adjustment (from Liberman 1989).

The following example shows how the model can be used. The example is based on an actual conversation:

James had regular meetings with a psychologist at an outpatient unit. The psychologist was worried that James had missed several meetings in a row. That very day James' mother called and said that James refused to talk to her and that she had been unable to get in contact with him for several days. She was worried that James' condition had worsened and wanted something to be done. Two clinicians from the outpatient unit went to see James. He would not answer when they rang the doorbell. The door was open, so they entered the house. James was sitting on a sofa in the living room, looking down and out. On seeing the staff he looked relieved. He explained that there were surveillance cameras in the bathroom and lavatory and someone was watching him and saw everything he was doing. So he did not dare to leave the house or answer the phone. To avoid using the toilet, James had abstained from food and drink for several days. He was listless and exhausted and had stomach aches. The clinicians wanted to take James to the local psychiatric hospital, but he would not go with them. He was absolutely confident that nothing was wrong with him. He said it was the others that had a problem, those spying on him. The staff could not leave James in that condition and started preparing for compulsory hospitalization. Then one of them asked James for a pen and paper. She drew a simplified version of the stress/vulnerability model [see Figure 1.4] and while doing this she interviewed James about different elements in the model.

Clinician: The first section deals with the vulnerability to becoming psychotic. Some people are more prone to becoming psychotic than others. What about you?

James: I have had psychotic episodes several times before, but this time it is not me who has got a problem, it's the people who are harassing me.

Clinician: OK. Let us move on to the next point – stress factors. It is like this, you see, if you have this kind of vulnerability and experience a lot of stress coming from your environment, then your chances of becoming psychotic increase. Have you had any stressful experiences lately?

James: Yes, I have, indeed. The neighbours had parties several nights running. Often after I'd gone to bed some drunken people knocked on my door trying to come in. They mistook my door for that of the neighbour. And it ruined my sleep for several nights. In addition my mother nagged over nothing.

Clinician: Well, now that you have told me this I can see you are vulnerable to becoming psychotic and at the same time you have had a lot of stress

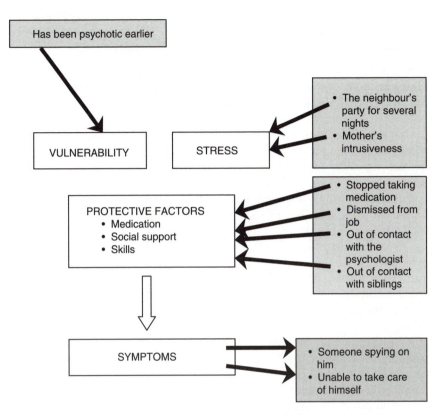

Figure 1.4 Simplified version of the stress/vulnerability model for use in interview.

in your environment. Now let us have a look at your protective factors. Protective factors are those that protect you from becoming psychotic. Are you taking your medication?

James: I stopped taking it about a year ago. Actually, I have never liked medicines. Now I don't take any.

Clinician: How is your social support? Are you in contact with support workers?

James: My job used to be an important support for me, but I was sacked due to a period of decline. Besides that I don't have contact with anyone. I do not feel up to seeing my psychologist or my siblings, because my mother would only interfere then.

Clinician: Finally I want to know how your personal skills are. Are you able to take care of yourself?

James: No, of course not. I am just sitting here holding my stomach. I don't even get up to wash myself.

Clinician: What can you tell from what I have written here?

James: Now I can see I have got that vulnerability and I have experienced a lot of stress and you have not been taking good enough care of me to prevent me from becoming psychotic. So, no wonder I am ill.

James packed a small suitcase and went voluntarily to the hospital. By taking account of the model he could allow himself to be admitted to the hospital so that his self-respect was not wounded.

Our experience is that patients relate to the model and they often do so more readily than the staff. The model is, therefore, very suitable for educating patients. Why admit James to hospital because someone was spying on him?

Compulsory admission could have been experienced as an assault and the long-term work, aimed at alliance building, could have been destroyed. The model helped James to understand in a systematic way what was happening to him so that he could ask for help. The model can also help the staff avoid using force towards patients unnecessarily (Bentsen 1993; Neuchterlein and Dawson 1984, both in Borchgrevink *et al.* 1999). When patients understand the model it gives them a feeling of having some control over the illness. This feeling of control is a condition for developing coping skills (Ursin 1984).

Aron Antonovsky stresses the importance of interpretation and understanding for coping (Antonovsky 1991). Stressors can be positive, negative or neutral and should not be automatically viewed as injurious to health. He identifies three mechanisms for coping with stressors: by redefining stressors as non-stressors; by avoiding stressors; or by 'winning over' the stressor. Education and social skills training can enable such situations to be reframed as non-stressful. Furthermore, the resultant self-confidence can work to reduce stress.

Antonovsky also introduced the concept of 'sense of coherence' (SOC). He states that SOC has significance in improving coping skills and that there is a clear connection between a person's SOC and health.

The sense of coherence consists of three elements:

- **Meaningfulness** – the person feels that life has meaning and is worth investing with engagement and feeling.
- **Comprehensibility** – the person manages to understand and appraise reality, and experiences the stimuli coming from the inner and outer world as predictable and understandable phenomena.
- **Manageability** – the world is perceived as manageable. The person feels that they possess the resources required to meet the challenges of life and its stressors or that such resources can be found in the close environment. (Antonovsky 1987)

Meaningfulness is the most important and most motivating factor in SOC. For a situation to be handled it should have meaning and value and, in addition, be understandable and predictable.

Both Liberman's stress/vulnerability–mastering competence model and Antonovsky's sense of coherence model support the idea that the coping capacity develops in the context of life experience and that lack of coping resources can be compensated, to a certain degree, by resources in the near surroundings. Knowledge and social support are examples of such resources.

Psychosis – what is it?
Jan Olav Johannessen

We often use complicated foreign words to describe mental disorders. 'Psychosis' is a foreign word. If we use such difficult terms it can easily lead to the assumption that the disorder is hard to understand. It may appear mystical. It is therefore important to keep in mind that we are dealing with the emotional and psychological problems that people experience. These are reactions that may affect anyone if the pressure is sufficiently strong. We use the term 'neurosis' to describe 'light' psychiatric problems and 'psychosis' for 'heavier' psychiatric problems.

In this section, we will try to explain what psychosis actually is.

Someone's behaviour may seem strange and cannot be described as 'normal'. A person may hear voices inside their head or be convinced that they are being persecuted or spied on. They may have sleep disturbance or start avoiding people or may experience emotions and reactions that are difficult to understand. These are just some of the symptoms that might enable us to diagnose psychosis.

The word psychosis may take on a personal meaning for some people. It is the description of behaviour that has confused and frightened us in some way and even made us angry. This diagnosis may produce a range of reactions. Sometimes it provides a sense of relief, because we know there is, at least, an explanation for the weird behaviour. Sometimes it produces a sense of loss and this feeling may often prove more intense than the sense of relief. The loss experienced is of someone who used to be happy, friendly and safe and seemed to have a bright future. But now this person is someone else, someone different – who may be sad, anxious, unpredictable and uncomfortable.

Sometimes relatives of a mentally sick person will feel guilty. They may ask: 'What have I done that may have caused this?'; 'What have I done wrong?'; 'If only I had been a better parent, brother, sister, son, daughter or friend, this might have never happened.' These reactions are quite common. But above all, they ask questions such as: 'What actually is psychosis?'; 'What causes psychosis?'; 'How shall we explain this to others?'; 'Is it inherited?'; 'How should it be treated?' and 'What happens to the sick person in the long run?'

The first question: what is psychosis?

To put it simply, psychosis is a condition of *confusion*. Basically, everyone can become so confused that their state may be covered by the term 'psychosis'. But this will depend on particular life situations and external stress factors, as well as the personality of the individual and their ability to cope with stresses.

Like many other medical expressions the term 'psychosis' has its origin in classical Greek, namely in the word: *psyche*, which means *mind* (as in *psychology* – the study of the mind) and the suffix *-osis*, which means *a state or condition of* (as in *thrombosis*, which literally means *a state of clotting*).

Such a condition of confusion does not emerge without reason. In nearly all cases the state of confusion or breakdown is preceded by a shorter or longer period of general signs, indicating some mental problems. These may include anxiety, uneasiness, sadness, lack of energy, isolation and other signs of mental illness. When these problems persist the mental stress increases and finally we have a total breakdown with confusion or psychosis as the next stage in the development of the illness.

The phase prior to psychotic breakdown is called the *warning phase* or the *prodromal phase*. After this the person will go through a shorter or longer period during which he gradually loses his grip on reality. This is a transitional phase which is characterized by a sense of the personality dissolving. This phase can be seen as a state of unreality.

It is possible for any of us to become seriously confused leading to a state of psychosis, i.e. anyone may break down if the pressure (stress) is strong enough. But what is stressful for me might not be stressful for you and vice versa. The way we cope with various kinds of stress has something to do with our personalities and early experiences. We, therefore, use the term *experienced stress* to explain what is of importance for the particular way in which individuals react.

When someone becomes ill like this and loses the sense of reality it is called a *psychotic episode*. People who have experienced it say that it is like losing control of oneself, becoming crazy or feeling that everything around is exploding (which may be a better description).

With the passage of time and effective treatment, people usually recover from psychotic episodes. For those experiencing a further episode, the period of feeling relatively well is called *remission*. Given adequate levels of support many of those who have only few psychotic episodes can lead a satisfactory life most of the time.

There are many kinds of psychosis

Psychotic symptoms may vary widely and they can even be experienced differently from one episode to another. The symptoms are affected differently by medication and they are reduced, in a varying degree, by treatment and between episodes. Psychosis can lead to changes in emotions, mood and ways of thinking and this may give rise to abnormal ideation, which often makes it difficult for others to understand the person's feelings. The term psychosis covers a number of related disorders (schizophrenia, bipolar disorder and others) (see Table 1.2).

Within the main groups there are large variations and different subgroups.

What are the symptoms of psychosis?

Symptoms are descriptions of significant changes indicating that we are not well. It is not always easy for psychotic people to identify the symptoms themselves, because the brain, which should recognize the symptoms, is actually the affected part of the body.

The core symptoms of psychosis could be described as a gradual decrease in the ability to differentiate oneself from the surroundings. Our psychological defences break down and we become unsure of who we are and of our surroundings (see Table 1.2). Each person's ability to function normally depends on being confident of who he/she is. When under pressure (what we have called *experienced pressure*) this ability (self-concept) breaks down and we may become a little, or seriously, confused. Based on this, we can explain

Table 1.2 Main types of psychosis

Reactive	Paranoid	Schizophrenia
• Major environmental stress • May affect anyone • Brief • Any age • Total recovery	• Limited range of symptoms • Delusions • Functioning ability remains • Onset: up to 50 years of age • Long lasting	• Hallucinations • Delusions • Impaired functioning • Affects young people • Long lasting
Manic depressive	**Schizoaffective**	**Organic**
• Changed self-esteem • Changes in mood • Changed activity • Affects young people and those up to the age of 50 • Periodic	• Both affective and schizophrenia symptoms • Impaired functioning • Affects young people • Fluctuating course • Long lasting	• Physical findings • Intoxication • Hormone imbalance • Illnesses • Any age

all the other symptoms in a logical way. In the case of increased stress, the mechanism of defence, which is our regular psychological strategy, is immobilized.

Common symptoms of psychosis are:

1   confused thinking
2   delusions
3   hallucinations
4   lack of motivation
5   changes in emotions.

In addition, the patient has other symptoms, such as anxiety, depression etc. which are symptoms all may experience when trying to overcome personal problems. But we must not forget that the most distinctive feelings and experiences are suffering, pain and despair. These symptoms always appear gradually, sometimes more quickly and sometimes more slowly.

Confused thinking

Everyday thoughts allowing us to lead a normal life may become confused and not make any sense. Some patients believe that others control their thoughts or can even read their minds.

The Greek philosopher Aristotle claimed that to think was to speak to oneself.

Our thoughts might be called the most personal aspects of ourselves, but where do they come from? If you are doing something and then suddenly something crosses your mind or if you start thinking of things you had not planned to think of – where do these thoughts come from? Is there some kind of thought-productive organ that you cannot control or do thoughts come from an unknown part of you? Who is thinking the thoughts that suddenly occur – is it you or some different part of you?

Reflections or speculations like these are absolutely normal and they have engaged many people – philosophers, for instance – for hundreds of years. When we are relaxed and feel secure about ourselves and our emotions, and have good relations with other people, then thoughts like this will not lead to any particular worries or problems. But when a person is under considerable stress or feels that he does not have control over his own 'self-relations', he might start to wonder about these things. Some may feel that they are 'staring' at their own thoughts and have a strange sense that the thoughts are not actually their own. Some experience having the kinds of thoughts which they want to disown or feel they 'shouldn't' think. These may be nasty or forbidden thoughts of a sexual or violent nature. If a person starts feeling this way about his own thoughts, this may be a prelude to thinking that the thoughts are not his own and they may be perceived as coming from other people, from

God or from the devil. Some may feel that others are stealing their thoughts or, on the contrary, are putting thoughts into their heads. If this persists over time it will often lead to the development of specific systems or delusions that help explain the weird experiences.

As a result of such thought disturbances, the person may have problems with making sense when talking, difficulties in concentrating, in following a conversation or in remembering things. The person's thoughts are jumbled. Some may be preoccupied with just one thought, and thereby reject others, or be obsessed with some minor details so that things are not seen as complete.

Delusions

The boundaries between me and the surroundings are blurred; it becomes impossible to separate what relates to me and what concerns others.

When a person experiences thought disturbances or has an inflexible self-concept over a period of time, he may develop what we call *delusions*. These are not always incorrect conceptions of the world or oneself, but rather 'distorted' ways of understanding things and events. They often have their own 'logic' which is difficult to contest.

The most important criterion that marks ideas out as delusional is their damaging effect on our relationships with others. In principle, we have to accept that others may have ideas about the world that we do not understand, but when a person's mental concepts make it hard for them to relate to others, to attend work or to live harmoniously in the family, leading to quarrels and conflicts, then it is the responsibility of psychiatry to help the person in trouble.

A delusion is a distorted interpretation which is not shared by other members of the same cultural background. The sick person is so convinced of the delusion that even the most logical counterevidence will not convince him otherwise. For instance, cars parked outside may make a patient think that he is being spied on by the CIA. Or he may be sitting in a train watching someone fold a newspaper and may suddenly take it into his head that this is a sign from above meaning he is chosen to give birth to a new Christ. We can see that the person in these examples misinterprets surrounding events and believes they refer to him. Perhaps the best example is of those people who believe they are being addressed from the TV screen and that what is going on on the screen refers directly to them.

Delusions come in various forms:

- *Paranoid delusion*:
  A false conviction of being spied on or singled out in a negative way.
- *Delusion of grandeur*:
  Conviction of one's having special power, being an important religious leader, politician or scientist.

- *Depressive delusion*:
  A strong belief that one is guilty of a terrible crime or is responsible for some gruesome events happening in the world.

Delusions can lead to bizarre behaviour. A person who believes that he is being watched by strangers may stay up all night and become very secretive. Another may be convinced that he has received a calling from God to lead people to the promised land and he may stop passers-by in order to recruit them. For some people, delusions may be rather harmless and even a source of comfort. For others, they may have serious far-reaching consequences and even create dangerous situations. A person who feels he is constantly being pursued may become suicidal.

Hallucinations

When the boundary between the self and the surroundings becomes blurred, it becomes difficult to differentiate between the present external stimuli (aural, olfactory or visual sensations) and those one believes oneself to be seeing, hearing, smelling or tasting, but which do not, actually, exist. The most common instance is of hearing voices that nobody else can hear. The person's own thoughts sound like voices inside their head or like voices from the outside.

Sometimes people with thought disturbances will feel that the thoughts they are thinking are not their own. From here it is a short way to presuming that something or someone is thinking the thoughts for them. Just imagine thinking a thought that is not your own! This may be experienced as someone else talking to you.

A person who is about to develop a psychosis sometimes has the sensation that he is hearing voices. At the outset or at certain times (in the evenings, for example), they are often taken for one's own thoughts. After a while, the sensations may become more persistent and the sick person may have such experiences for much of the time. The voices can be nagging, offending or even funny. They can ask the person to do certain things, comment (often in a critical manner) on what he is doing or repeat the same thoughts aloud. Many patients shout at the voices or laugh at the funny things they hear.

While some people hear voices occasionally, others hear them almost constantly. And while most patients feel uncomfortable when hearing such voices, some may find them friendly and feel that they provide them with a sense of security.

Seeing things which are not really there (visual hallucinations) is less common. This occurs most often when the psychosis is caused by substance abuse. Gustatory (taste) hallucinations may also occur and a strange taste of food can make a paranoid person believe someone is trying to poison him. Tactile hallucinations may also take place. Hallucinations are often interpreted as real by those having them, and may become entirely convincing to very ill patients. Therefore, it is not surprising that hallucinations can lead to intense agitation and high anxiety.

Hallucinations develop gradually, from an initial feeling of uncertainty to absolute conviction.

Poor motivation

Poor motivation or lack of it can be either *primary*, which reveals itself as lack of interest in things, as withdrawal or as reduced activity, or *secondary*, where it is a consequence of other symptoms of psychosis. Sometimes we underestimate or forget this. We need to remember that it is not listlessness, laziness or lack of will that causes poor motivation. Most often it is due to an endless feeling of hopelessness, fatigue, anxiety and some kind of paralysis of the ability to think clearly.

As a result the sick person will often withdraw from family, friends, colleagues or neighbours. He or she may become very sluggish and some spend the whole day in front of the television. Everyday things, such as getting up in the morning or doing the dishes, seem impossible. This will often cause irritation and become a source of strain for others.

Consequently, when we encourage a patient to get up and do something, it is important to remember that poor or absent motivation is caused by the illness and should not be accounted for by laziness or lack of initiative.

Changed emotions

Another symptom that is often connected with psychosis is a change in the way one feels, often with no obvious reason. A psychotic episode often starts with a change in mood. Sometimes the spirits may go up, but most often the patient feels down. Eventually the feelings are most likely to become flat – the person feels lower than usual or shows fewer emotions or interest in what is going on around him.

It is important to be aware that the feelings or emotions have not disappeared, but that the patient withdraws from contact with the outer world in order to avoid undesirable emotional experiences.

Important events may be accepted with indifference. Some may have inappropriate reactions, such as, for instance, giggling when receiving bad news. To put it another way, when a person's emotions become overwhelming, when the strain gets too big, this may result in psychosis.

Chapter 2

Methods

Psychoeducational multifamily group model
Anne Lise Øxnevad

The intention of Chapter 1 was to give the reader some background information about psychosis. The model of stress/vulnerability that has been described is among the themes we teach patients' families during seminars, to enhance their understanding of psychosis. In this book, we concentrate on psychoeducational multifamily work with psychotic patients, since this is the group of patients from which we have derived our experience. We do, however, recognize that this model may also be applied to other disturbances such as affective and eating disorders.

Family work consists of the following:

For relatives:
- presentations about the crisis consequent on the illness
- drawing a genogram/family tree
- detecting early warning signs and possible signs of relapse.

For the patient:
- presentation of family work, its contents and purpose
- getting to know each other
- detecting early warning signs of possible relapse.

For everyone:
- An **educational seminar** for all the families participating, during a full Saturday or over two evenings.
- **Multifamily group meetings**: five families meet every other week for 90-minute sessions during at least 2 years. There are two family group leaders in each group.
- The **first multifamily group meeting**: introduction of all group members.
- The **second multifamily group meeting**: participants describe how the close relatives' illness has affected them.

- The **following multifamily group meetings** over the next 2 years: the **problem-solving method**.

This can be implemented in different ways, depending on the patient's and the family's situation and the healthcare service they are involved with. If the patient stays in a psychiatric institution or is registered at an outpatient department then he may be contacted through the patient's individual therapist. Even at this point, the foundation of good cooperation with the patient's individual therapist should be laid, since this will eventually promote the teamwork aimed at achieving the same goal. The same holds true where the patient stays in contact with a psychiatric centre.

If the patient is under the care of the health services of the local district then it is natural that contact should be made there. Of course, psychoeducational multifamily groups may be arranged in primary healthcare service settings as well as in specialised healthcare services – where necessary, the two services may cooperate in the work.

William McFarlane's multifamily model is based on the principle that the patient is a participant in the group. The patient is initially asked if the rest of the family should participate. This is to take account of situations where there is no regular contact with the family.

Invitation to family work
Anne Lise Øxnevad

How to engage the families

The family is invited to join the group with the patient. When we use the term 'family' we mean the patient's close relatives, their spouse/live-in partner, parents and siblings over 18 years of age. But other relatives, for example, grandparents, foster parents or others who are considered to be close to the patient, may be included as well.

The age limit for siblings is determined individually in every case and sometimes the limit of 18 years can be lowered, in the light of the sibling's maturity, intellect, and significance for the patient. Siblings also need information and help to support the ill family member. Younger siblings or children should not be treated as potential supporters of the patient, but they should receive answers to any questions they may have concerning the patient's illness. The group leader may need to decide who is responsible for making such links.

The first contact

The initial engagement with the family may take various pathways depending on the location of family and patient, as well as on their specific links with their healthcare service. If the patient is in an inpatient unit at a psychiatric institution or is registered at an outpatient clinic, it is natural for the first contact to go through the patient's individual therapist. It is important from the start to build a good relationship between the individual therapist and the family group leaders to ensure a common strategy and common goals. Where the patient is linked to the community healthcare service through a psychiatric nurse or a general practitioner, this is where the contact starts. Psychoeducational multifamily groups, can, of course, be run in the community as well as in hospitals or, indeed, in combination and cooperation.

Where should the first meeting be held?

If the patient is hospitalized the meeting can be held in the hospital. Alternatively, it may be held at an outpatient department or in the individual therapist's office. Sometimes it might be appropriate to hold it at the family's/patient's home. Some families may find this a positive move since it gives them a sense that their own situation is being seriously addressed. Nevertheless, in most cases the first meeting is held in an office at, say, an outpatient unit.

From the outset, it is important for the family and the patient to view the group leader as a collaborative colleague, so that relationships may be free of tension. After introductions, some small talk about traffic, weather, parking conditions is a common icebreaker. Such informal talk helps to convey genuine interest in the family. We go on to indicate that the group leaders want to be a support to them and are keen to work with the family by communicating knowledge and advice on how to deal with the illness. It should be stressed that the family is an important resource for the patient and that the programme will give them resources for dealing with day-to-day problems. In many cases, the invitation to family work is misinterpreted. They may feel that the therapist is viewing the family as the cause of the illness and that they themselves need treatment. Some family members can be extremely sceptical when entering the process, so it is very important to stress that such a negative view of the family should not be taken. We look on the family as a resource, not a cause of the illness. This resource may be overloaded and under strain, and the intervention process is designed to help them. They are our co-workers.

It is not uncommon for family members to offload their frustrations by attacking the healthcare services. It is important to listen and show respect for their feelings and situation. Through empathy and supportive attitudes the group leaders provide them with a wider picture of family work. It is important to explain the basic concept of psychoeducation. Of course, education and training have, for years, been offered to families experiencing physical healthcare problems. Families with diabetic children have been given training in how to deal with that condition. Psychiatry, by way of contrast, has not offered the same kind of help, even though it has long been known that these patients and their relatives need similar inputs from specialist services on the consequences and treatment of psychosis. Today, with easy access to the internet, many patients and their families have developed a growing interest in research on the illness. The group leader will present to the families the results of current research in this field. This may give the family a better knowledge base for dealing with the illness. However, some patients in this meeting will appear sceptical. They may be filled with anxiety and restlessness and wonder how they will endure a 90-minute meeting. Group leaders should always be tolerant and respond with open attitudes, such as, 'Just come and see how it is' or 'Just come for a while'. It is important to give the patient freedom to test things out. Many patients are also fearful when it comes to talking in groups. It is important to explain to them that they do not need to say anything until they feel it safe to do so. Sometimes the patient is in hospital or is too ill to attend this first meeting with the family. It is important then to impart the same information to the patient at a point where they can take it in.

Some families are doubtful whether or not they should attend the group meetings. It is therefore important for the group leaders to convey the results of research, which indicate that the prognosis is far better when the family and the patient have participated in a psychoeducation process. Sometimes the family needs more time for discussion among themselves before they can make any decision. In such cases the family is given a new appointment, and further time to reach a decision. The group leader takes the initiative here. Not all families are able to sort things out, especially at this phase. During the first phase of the illness, the family is in crisis, with a host of distressing thoughts and feelings to address. Some families may be concerned by the commitment needed to join groups that run for 2 years. It should be explained to them that for the first year the goal is to prevent relapse, while during the next year the focus is on rehabilitation. A common initial feeling among families is that a 2-year period seems very long; but 2 years later many families do not want the group meetings to end.

First contact: dealing with the crisis
Anne Lise Øxnevad

What is a crisis?

A crisis is a limited period of time of mental imbalance in a person who faces a difficult problem that they, at the current time, can neither run from nor resolve using their usual problem solving skills.

(Caplan 1964)

Such a crisis may occur when someone, or their close relative, becomes affected with a serious illness. Normal reactions may be feelings of unreality, denial, despair, anxiety, dizziness, upset stomach, rumination, guilt, anger, weeping, and sleep disturbances. This may also lead to reduced problem-solving ability.

Review of the crisis following the illness

In the first part of the introductory conversations with the family, we review the crisis the relatives have experienced since the family member became psychotic. If necessary, this may be discussed in further conversations at a later stage. The purpose of doing this is to let each family member work through their own reaction to the relative's breakdown. By going back in time and finding out when the family first noticed changes in the patient, we start a process that makes possible reflection and processing of the experience. In some patients, there may have been a gradual onset to the changes in behaviour and it may therefore be difficult for the family to tell precisely when the illness commenced. Other families may have experienced some recent dramatic events. If the ill family member is hospitalized, the family's experience of the crisis may be different from their memory of any earlier crises.

Many relatives have had to live through the patient's symptoms for some time before he or she received treatment. Relatives are often unfamiliar with the symptoms of psychosis and may delay considerably before contacting a doctor. They may have struggled for some time and tried to get help without success. Relatives may often be desperate for help in dealing with the patient's symptoms and this may last for some time before they contact the health services so that, by this stage, they are often exhausted.

The initial help the family receives from the health services will largely determine how well they handle the crisis. It will, of course, also be of considerable help if there is a network of relatives and friends to support them through all the difficult experiences and emotions they may encounter.

Many relatives refer to feelings of frustration after meeting with the hospital staff. They are surprised that those at the hospital are often uninterested in the information they could provide at the point of hospitalization. The sense of being rejected and ignored, the feeling that nobody is interested in what they believe to be important information about the patient and their situation prior to the hospitalization is described as hard to bear by many relatives. Many parents are also upset if they are not offered follow-up counselling for the stress they experience where they have struggled to have their son or daughter admitted and the outcome was an involuntary admission, perhaps with assistance from the police.

Another example of frustration experienced by some relatives is where help is not made available because the patient will not acknowledge that they are ill, refuses to accept any help offered or may be not 'sufficiently ill' to meet the criteria for compulsory admission. Another recurring theme is of relatives wanting information from the hospital which they fail to receive.

The 'crisis conversation' – or conversations, if necessary – is important because it provides the relatives with an opportunity to recount what they have felt and experienced in connection with a family member's illness. They often have thoughts and worries they need to air and want answers to many questions.

For the group leaders it is important to listen to the family's experiences and offer them support for the criticism and frustration they might be feeling towards the health services.

Even though it may be easy to understand what a colleague has thought or done, it is still important for members of the team not to become defensive. It is also important to be able to admit that everyone may make mistakes and that staff do not always measure up to expectations.

If the events occurring around the breakout of illness are not adequately reviewed and worked through, it is our experience that these themes will reappear at a number of points in the family group. In a way, the family is stuck in the crisis. If this happens, the family should be offered more 'crisis conversations' until the crisis is worked through thoroughly. This is done separately for each family, as these are subjects which cannot be discussed in the multifamily group.

If a family experiences a crisis after the family groups have been started, separate conversations should always be offered. Separate conversations are also offered in situations where there are problems that cannot be put off or cannot be solved in the group.

Second contact: mapping the genealogical chart
Anne Lise Øxnevad

The next step in the programme is to explore the social network and resources of the family. In psychiatric treatment it may be useful to draw up a family tree or *genogram*. Drawing up a family tree helps the family better understand its internal relationships and provides a structured and lucid insight into the family and its significant life events. The knowledge that emerges from this activity will be of great importance in working with the family towards the rehabilitation of the patient. The family culture, religion, political stand-point, traditions, names, illnesses, etc. – these constitute the linking material that is passed on from generation to generation. In the history of the family, we come across both positive and negative events whose importance may persist to the present. A genealogical chart is a graphical family tree describing the structure and relationships of the family for two or more generations. It reveals how the family members are connected to each other – both across generations and between individuals within the same family.

In the family tree, we can associate information such as name, gender and marital status with significant events that took place in the family, such as births, marriages, divorces and deaths. The purpose of collecting this information is to reveal any hereditary traits, attain an overview of relationships that are supportive or distressing and learn about important events within the family. If a relationship is marked as tense, we must be sensitive to the risk of high *expressed emotion*.

This approach is an effective way of asking about hereditary traits because by drawing a genogram we get information both about positive happenings within the family and things that proved stressful. The family can talk about the strains they have experienced, that have not lead to any illness, but which they have handled successfully. Focusing on both resources and problems is an essential feature of the model and is emphasized throughout the work.

We endeavour not to direct the questions solely on problems but, instead, try to ask about 'events'. When we suspect there has been a stressful period, for instance, births close together, deaths, house moves, etc., we try to comment on this in a positive, empathic and caring way, seeking to validate and reinforce the family's coping strategies. Overlapping events like deaths, illnesses and moving are indicators of considerable stress, of which the family is often unaware. The family will experience this kind of interpretation as supportive leading to the establishment of a positive working alliance.

The quality of relationships should be examined and we need to enquire who gets along well with whom and if there are any problematic relationships. We need also to establish the patient's closest relationship. Comments should aim to be supportive. If the family members disagree on how to describe a particular relationship, it is important to respect both viewpoints. Relationships can be experienced differently, from a variety of perspectives, both within and outside the family itself.

In this connection, it is important to raise the question about who should participate in the family group. Parents, spouse, friend/partner and siblings above 18 may normally take part. In addition, other persons the patient is close to may participate. This is also the right time to discuss who of the family members should be invited to the educational seminar. The family should be given a copy of the genealogical tree after it has been completed. The session should end with informal conversation.

The most common symbols used for drawing a genogram are shown in Figure 2.1.

Third contact: monitoring early warning signs
Trond Grønnestad

During a family conversation, we will try to discover the patient's individual warning signs that may signal relapse. If the patient is well enough, he or she may participate in the conversation.

The core task of all psychoeducational family work is to teach the family and the patient about the illness and how to cope with it. One of the most important coping strategies is to recognize the early signs the patient shows

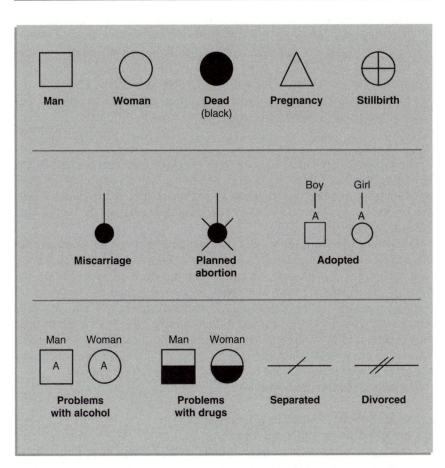

Figure 2.1 Icons and symbols most commonly used in a genogram.

when the situation is worsening. Most patients and relatives will confirm that they notice some changes in the patient before the symptoms emerge.

In 1998 Smeby *et al.* conducted a survey where 11 patients were asked the following questions:

1   Did you have any thoughts or feelings that made you believe you were relapsing again?
2   What did you do when you had these thoughts or feelings?

When answering the first question, 81% of the patients stated they were able to describe changes in their symptoms and behaviour which they interpreted as a pre-warning of relapse.

As to the second question, Smeby writes:

From the descriptions we see that the patients often feel that something is wrong and try to do something to overcome the bad feelings and thoughts. They use different strategies to lessen, divert and/or remove what they experience as signs of impairment. During this period it is possible to reach most of them through collaborative help. Thereafter the psychosis passes a threshold where the patient no longer has control, but is constrained by some inner processes, which now dominate.

(Smeby *et al.* 1998)

These changes are called *warning signs of relapse* and they are early signs indicating that the patient is about to get worse. Most symptoms will have early signs or warning signals prior to the recurrence of psychosis. These can be present weeks or days before the symptoms emerge (see the list that follows, on page 36).

In scientific literature, the terms *prodromes* and *warning signs of relapse* are often used as synonyms. This is not accurate. Warning signs of relapse are early symptoms that indicate a relapse. Warning signs are identified on the basis of the experience from the earlier psychotic episodes. The phase of warning signs will appear prior to each psychotic episode. A patient's prodromes can resemble or be identical to the warning signs, but the patient can only experience the prodromes once and that is during the prodromal phase. This is the phase with which the illness begins. At this stage, the patient has not yet experienced a psychotic breakdown (see the following list).

The most common prodromes are:

- marked social isolation or withdrawal
- marked deficiency in social roles
- markedly strange behaviour (collecting strange things, hoarding, talking to oneself in public places)
- obvious failure to maintain personal hygiene
- vague or flat emotional behaviour
- vague or circumstantial speech or marked reduction of speech (speech disturbance)
- strange religious beliefs, magical thinking and strange ideas such as telepathy, clairvoyance and ideas of reference
- perceptual disturbances
- marked lack of initiative, interest or energy. (TIPS research protocol 1996)

When the patient receives treatment early and has experienced only one psychotic episode, he has not yet experienced warning signs of relapse. The signs he had prior to the psychotic breakdown were prodromes. We will, however, choose to treat these signs in the same way as we do warning signs of relapse.

There has not yet been any research conducted on whether prodromes can appear later as warning signals of relapse, but clinical experience suggests that the most obvious prodromes will be found among the warning signals of relapse. (Note: research is now being conducted on this in connection with the TIPS project.)

In the following we will consistently use the term *warning signs* even though this will denote *prodromes* in some cases.

When explaining the term *warning signs* to the family it may be useful to make a comparison with flu. Having flu is something most people have experienced and is, therefore, easy to understand. We ask the family if they notice anything before flu breaks out. Most will then mention signs like sore throat, listlessness, cold, fatigue for no obvious reason etc. These are early signs or warning signals that flu is on the way. In the same way psychosis exhibits warning signals that will appear before the disease itself breaks out. Examples of this will be sleep disturbance, increased irritability, lack of interest etc. When we discover that flu is on the way, we take some precautions. We slow down a bit, go to bed earlier, take vitamins etc. in order to try and avoid the flu developing or, at worst, to prevent its being as serious as it might otherwise be.

The same holds true with warning signals of psychosis relapse. When we recognize these, there is still some possibility of controlling the illness. If the patient or those close to the patient notice some warning signals, then efforts can be aimed at avoiding or at least reducing the symptoms. For instance, the patient can be protected from environmental stress or protective factors initiated such as medication, social support etc. Early admission to a psychiatric hospital can be considered as one of the interventions that may limit the development of the illness.

To provide greater reassurance for the family during the interview and, at the same time, to ensure that the most essential warning signals are clearly registered, we have developed a checklist (see Figure 2.2).

Forms for relatives

The checklist includes 35 warning signs of relapse, of which the family may only recognize eight–10. The warning signals are found in the *only before I become ill* column. In the *often* column we find *persistent symptoms*. These are symptoms that last for some time and will not disappear even if the patient takes medication. Persistent symptoms can vary in intensity. Whispering voices, high levels of suspicion or finding no joy in life – these are examples of such symptoms.

To avoid offending the patients we explain that we do not believe they have all the warning signals contained in the list – we are using it as a comprehensive checklist. After we have completed the list we ask if there are any warning signs of relapse missing from the list and if there are any other things the patient notices before getting ill.

1 Rarely
2 Only before I get ill
3 Often

Please tick the points that are applicable. The warning signals will be
listed in the 'only before I get ill' column.

	1	2	3
1. Are you feeling tense or nervous?	❑	❑	❑
2. Are you feeling depressed?	❑	❑	❑
3. Do you have problems sleeping?	❑	❑	❑
4. Are you feeling restless?	❑	❑	❑
5. Do you have any difficulties with concentration?	❑	❑	❑
6. Don't enjoy life?	❑	❑	❑
7. Have you got a poor appetite?	❑	❑	❑
8. Any problems with remembering things?	❑	❑	❑
9. Do you feel persecuted?	❑	❑	❑
10. Do you see less of your friends?	❑	❑	❑
11. Do you feel ridiculed?	❑	❑	❑
12. Do you lack interest in the things around you?	❑	❑	❑
13. Do you ruminate over religious problems?	❑	❑	❑
14. Do you feel unwell for no obvious reason?	❑	❑	❑
15. Do you feel in higher spirits than usual?	❑	❑	❑
16. Do you hear voices that nobody else can hear?	❑	❑	❑
17. Do you see anything that nobody else can see?	❑	❑	❑
18. Do you feel inferior?	❑	❑	❑
19. Do you lack interest in doing anything?	❑	❑	❑
20. Do you care less about the way you are dressed?	❑	❑	❑
21. Do you have little hope for the future?	❑	❑	❑
22. Do you have bad dreams?	❑	❑	❑
23. Are you more aggressive than usual?	❑	❑	❑
24. Are you more easily annoyed over trifling matters?	❑	❑	❑
25. Do you have thoughts of hurting yourself or committing suicide?	❑	❑	❑
26. Do you often have aches or pains?	❑	❑	❑
27. Have you thought of hurting or killing others?	❑	❑	❑
28. Do you drink alcohol or take drugs?	❑	❑	❑
29. Does it feel as if parts of you body were changing?	❑	❑	❑
30. Does the environment seem strange or unreal?	❑	❑	❑
31. Do you sleep more than usual?	❑	❑	❑
32. Do people say that you are acting differently?	❑	❑	❑
33. Do you find it easy to set off an argument?	❑	❑	❑
34. Are you losing/gaining weight?	❑	❑	❑
35. Do you think others want to hurt you?	❑	❑	❑

Figure 2.2 Common warning signs prior to psychosis.

On identifying the warning signs of relapse we ask the patient, together with the family, to point out the most distinctive warning signs of relapse – limited to those that they are most sure of. (A selection of warning signals is described at length elsewhere in this volume.)

If the patient participates in this conversation, the relatives have a chance of asking about some things they may not have dared to ask earlier due to fear of negative reaction from the patient. Our experience shows that there will usually be a dialogue about the warning signs of relapse between the patient and the relatives as the checklist is worked through.

As an example of this, the checklist contains the following question: 'Do you have thoughts about hurting yourself or committing suicide?' Relatives who have experienced suicide attempts or threats of suicide from the patient are despairing, worried and angry. This may present their first opportunity to ask the patient questions about this.

A father asked once: 'What do you want us to do when you say that you want to end your life?' The family had a useful discussion on the subject. Since this was a subject they had not been able to touch on, they had become stuck in a rut. The patient was having a hard time and often felt that life was not worth living. He expressed this to his mother. This resulted in the parents, especially the father, policing the patient. The patient, who had already been somewhat suspicious of everybody, became totally paranoid towards his father. During the discussion, he was able to confirm that at times he had thought his father would kill him because of this tight control.

One condition that should be kept in mind when airing such difficult subjects is that the relatives should have had enough time to overcome the crisis. If the family is still sitting on strong feelings, this could prove hard for the patient. Thus it is the group leader's responsibility to monitor amd steer the conversation so that the emerging feelings are not excessive.

Three copies are made of the list of specific warning signals. One copy is for the relatives, one for the patient and one for the group leader. It is also important that the group leader know the patient's warning signs of relapse. This is particularly important for 'first-timers'.

When the family is over the worst crisis and is getting back to normal, both the relatives and the patient tend to try to ignore the warning signs of relapse when they appear. It is, therefore, important that the group leader should be familiar with the warning signals and be able to draw the family's attention to them when they do appear.

Contact between group leader and patient
Anne Lise Øxnevad

In addition to the whole family meeting, the individual patients each have meetings with the group leader. The duration of these meetings may vary depending on the phase of the illness. The group leader needs to contact the patient's individual therapist and ask whether the patient is now ready for contact and, if not, to ascertain when the patient will be ready for the first meeting. The meeting involves building an alliance and showing empathy. Building an alliance is of paramount importance in meeting the patient. The main purpose will be to help the patient to get to know the group leader and see him/her as a sympathetic person taking genuine interest in the patient.

It is the group leader who is the initiator of the conversation and should spend enough time on preliminary informal conversation to establish contact. The group leader should try to reach the patient through the patient's interests in, for instance, music, sports, books etc. The group leader should also inform the patient about what psychoeducational family work involves. Some patients become sceptical when they learn that so many people will attend group meetings. It is, therefore, very important that the group leader should explain that in these groups much emphasis is placed on creating a secure, consistent and relaxed atmosphere. The patients should be informed that the group leader will cooperate with the patient's individual therapist, but that this contact is, of course, bound by professional confidentiality. In one of the individual meetings with the patient, the warning signs of relapse should be mapped.

The meeting with the patient is shorter than that with the whole family. It usually takes about 30 minutes. The patient's condition will also clearly be taken into account.

Sometimes it may be difficult to get the patient to join the multifamily group. Some patients say they are sceptical about taking part in a group with others. The group leader should explain then that it is fine for the patient not to say anything, especially in the initial phase. Patients will often be in great doubt whether they should join the group. Some are afraid of being with other people, some are afraid to talk:

Peter: I don't think I can do this, it sounds scary.
Group leader: It feels scary because you don't know what it's like. I suggest that you don't make a decision yet, but join us for one meeting only to see what it is like. And you can decide later.
Peter: Yes, that doesn't sound so scary. But how can I stay there for one and a half hours?
Group leader: You stay as long as you manage; we are pleased that you're prepared to try.

Such an open and confidence-inspiring approach can be of vital importance in encouraging patients to participate in a multifamily group. Curiosity is aroused and patients are able to make their own choice after meeting the rest of the group. Experience shows that most of those participating in the first group meeting will return.

The relatives of the four to five families that will comprise the group have already met during the educational day and, therefore, they are not complete strangers when they come together at the first group meeting. This is not, however, the case with the patients. For them, this is their first meeting with the families and the other patients.

It can also be helpful to bring patients together for a joint meeting before starting the regular group meetings. This often enables them to join the multi-family groups. Patients could be invited to an educational evening where the theme could be 'What is psychosis?'. This would offer them an opportunity to discuss the theme among themselves. They often feel a need to talk to each other about common experiences in psychosis. Another kind of gathering could be a 'get together' with snacks and lemonade. A third possibility is to gather patients for a social activity, bowling, for instance. Such events offer patients the possibility of building a common network and, later on, to establish contact outside the group meetings as well.

The educational seminar
Trond Grønnestad

After at least three meetings with each family an educational seminar is arranged. This is based on the work seminar described in chapter 3 in *Schizophrenia and the Family* (Anderson *et al.* 1986). The purpose of the seminar is to provide information about psychosis and how the family can best manage the illness.

During the last 20 years the role of the family as the main caregiver to the ill person has been growing in importance. This trend has accompanied the closing down of large psychiatric institutions. At the same time, provision of information and support for families by the health services has been restricted. This has applied throughout the entire western world:

> Many therapists still fail to inform the patient or the family about the illness, its treatment and how the treatment system is organised. The family members might be shown sympathy, but they are rarely given information that can help them develop efficient means to deal with difficult behaviour on the part of the patient. Thus they are often unable to handle the patient's problems when he or she is discharged from hospital, when only partly recovered.
>
> What is ironic is that when problems with the patient arise at home, the health services often blame the family. This creates a spiral of blame and misunderstanding between the family and the health services.
>
> The therapists argue that the information might be upsetting and thus discouraging to the family. However, most families claim that not knowing anything about the illness is worse than having the information, no matter how serious the illness and prognosis might be. No professional

has all the answers, So far no one has been able to say that if you do **x**, the patient will not have a relapse or that if you do **y** he will have a relapse. Still it is possible to start sharing with the family the things we do know.

(Anderson et al. 1986: 73)

A father in one of our multifamily groups said at a group meeting: 'What frustrates us most is that we do not know if what we are doing for our daughter is right. We don't know whether or not we are following the treatment protocol. Sometimes I have wondered if I'm sabotaging the treatment protocol without ever knowing it.'

One of the problems health service workers face when talking to relatives about serious mental illnesses is that there are many things we do not know:

- We do not know exactly why this particular patient has fallen ill.
- We cannot say for sure what treatment will bring relief to the patient.
- And, finally, we cannot give a precise prognosis.

All the questions that we cannot answer might add to our refusal to provide information about the illness and how it could best be managed. But as Anderson *et al.* say: 'It is possible to start sharing what we know with the families.'

When someone in a family becomes mentally ill (whatever the condition), most families will try to help by being supportive, concerned, tolerant and caring for the person who is in trouble. For patients suffering from, for instance, schizophrenia, these normal responses which are usually helpful in the case of other illnesses will only make things worse. Too much forethought and caring, too much leniency and relaxed boundaries (which may be normal with other illnesses) seem to exacerbate the symptoms and trigger inappropriate behaviour. Anxious, disorganized and unmotivated patients need a milieu with clearly defined limits and a certain interpersonal distance between the patient and the rest of the family. It is therefore very important that the family should get information and help which would enable them to deal with the new and extensive task they are facing. There are several ways of providing information to relatives:

- **Written information** (information folders available in English from Psykiatrisk Opplysningsfond ProPsy International), see *www.psykopp.no*.
- **Series of multifamily group gatherings** (Plummeret *et al.* 1981, Zelitch 1980, both in Jordal and Repål 1999).
- **One-day educational seminar** (Anderson *et al.* 1986; McFarlane 1983).

Of those methods just mentioned we opted for the last approach and we also chose to have the seminar without patients present. Prior to the TIPS project the method had been tested on four multifamily groups – three groups in Stavanger and one group in Oslo. We had debated whether the patient should participate in the educational seminar or not; to test the alternatives, we chose to include the patients in the seminars held in Stavanger, while only the relatives were invited in Oslo. The subsequent evaluation demonstrated that many patients failed to attend the seminar held in Stavanger. Among those who did go, many felt there was too much information to cope with and thus made little use of the tuition (all the relatives found the tuition very useful). In Oslo, a constructive dialogue between the relatives and the presenter developed. This was difficult in Stavanger. Afterwards the relatives said that there were a lot of things they meant to ask but it was difficult with the patients present. (Our findings are supported by Anderson *et al.* 1986: 75.)

The education day comes relatively early in the course of a psychotic episode, at a time when it it is likely be difficult for the patient to tolerate as much stimuli as a full-day seminar involves.

Even patients who stabilize relatively early often have neither the energy nor the capacity to stay concentrated for a full day so early in the treatment course.

We have also found that, at this stage, the family members need to talk about their own worries without the patient present.

In the TIPS project we therefore chose to have the education seminar in the patients' absence.

A year after the groups have started a new 'top-up' seminar is arranged. This time the patient *is* present. It has proved difficult to assemble all the families for a full education day. In those groups where it was not possible we split the seminar over two nights.

The two group leaders conduct the seminar and are responsible for most of the lecturing. It is important to prepare thoroughly. We have benefited from inviting colleagues to help us with the lectures. It is an advantage to have psychiatrists who can talk about medication and possible side effects; it is also useful to have social workers present to talk about financial allowances. The professional content of the seminar is so broad that it is impossible for the same presenter to be a specialist in all subjects and answer all the questions that may arise.

It is important that the group leader should not attempt to deal with topics with which he/she is unfamiliar. This is easily seen through and it is easy to lose the group's confidence. If a group leader cannot answer a question it is OK to say: 'I don't think I know enough about this subject, but I will talk to someone who does, and give you a proper answer next time we meet.'

The group leader has also got an important task as a host to the relatives. This is the first time the families participating in the same multifamily group will meet. Some relatives may be nervous about having to talk or answer questions. Others may find it difficult to disclose to others that they have a son or a daughter who is ill.

Some of this insecurity is removed by creating a 'learning environment'. The group leaders take charge of the situation from the outset by introducing themselves and the lecturers. Then each of the family members is asked to introduce him- or herself and say a few words about their relationship with the patient. Every family receives a folder containing the agenda together with information brochures.

After the folders are handed out we go through the agenda for the day. Midway through the programme we have a 1-hour lunch break, where the families can talk together and get to know each other. This situation needs careful handling. For many of the families, this is their first opportunity to talk openly with others who are in the same difficult situation.

The group leaders and the other lecturers should sit at the same tables so that everyone has the opportunity to talk to them. As our experience shows, the conversation around the lunch table will concentrate on the subjects that have been covered during the lecture. The families readily appreciate the relevance of these subjects and will often have a number of questions or stories they want to share (see Table 2.1). Placing the group leaders one at each table

Table 2.1 Educational seminar subjects and example programme

Education subjects	Example of a programme for an educational seminar
• Crisis theories • Understanding psychosis • Different psychotic symptoms • Intoxication/psychosis • Warning signals on relapse • Stress/vulnerability model • Treatment • Psychotherapy • Milieu therapy • Medication • Family work • Rehabilitation • The law concerning mental health work • Professional secrecy	10:00–10:45 Presentation of the group leaders, the lecturers and the group members. Distribution of the written material and a short discussion of the subjects on the agenda Crisis theories 11:00–11:45 Understanding psychosis and stress vulnerability model 12:00–12:45 Different psychoses and different psychotic symptoms 12:45–13:45 Lunch 13:45–14:30 Warning signals of relapse Intoxication and psychosis 14:45–15:30 Treatment The law concerning mental health service Professional secrecy

helps reduce some of the families' insecurity. The group leader is a 'safe' person whom everyone in the group has come to know through the opening lectures. As hosts, one of the tasks that the group leaders should assume is to ensure that all the group members are involved in the conversation, and that everyone feels as comfortable as possible.

While families often accept the invitation to the educational seminar, they are uncertain about participating in a multifamily group (these are often the families that need that help most of all). The way these families are received and their opinion of the seminar will determine whether or not they will take part in a multifamily group later.

At the end of the seminar everyone is thanked for participating. The members are told when the first multifamily group meetings will be arranged and all the group members are encouraged to come.

The subjects covered at the lecture on this day will form the basis for the family's understanding of the illness and how they will manage it. During later group gatherings, we will repeatedly return to these subjects. It is therefore very important that the groups participating in the multifamily groups should attend the seminar.

The programme is comprehensive and the families will later need revision and a more thorough presentation. We have had positive experiences where group meetings have been presented as pure education. On such occasions the patients also take part. The patients have often been very active during these education meetings which are kept short in order to maintain concentration.

On occasions we invite along colleagues who have specialist knowledge of such subjects as medication, side effects, intoxication and psychosis.

One of the purposes of this treatment model is to enable the family to manage the illness in the best way possible. *To do this they need considerable information and knowledge.*

After the group has been running for a year another educational seminar is arranged. All the group leaders, patients and relatives take part in this seminar. Some of the issues and information presented at this seminar will be repeated from the previous one, but this time greater emphasis will be placed on the theme of *rehabilitation*.

Before the seminar we ask the group if there are particular subjects they would like to focus on. Quite often the families want more information about intoxication and psychosis. Subjects to be covered during this day may, for example, include:

- understanding psychosis
- stress/vulnerability model
- treatment, with emphasis on rehabilitation
- intoxication and psychosis.

Group structure and framework
Anne Lise Øxnevad

Knowledge-based multifamily work is built on the model by McFarlane. The model includes three steps:

1   Introductory conversations with family and the patient.
2   Educational seminar.
3   Multifamily group running for 2 years.

Each multifamily group consists of four to six families and two group leaders, meeting every second week for 2 years. The group is closed, but families or individuals may drop out and re-enter. If the group gets too small – where many participants have dropped out – a new family may be included. The new family must have participated in an educational seminar before joining the group, for instance, by attending the educational seminar held for another group. When a new family joins an existing group, the first two meetings of that group are repeated, that is, the meeting where the group members get acquainted with each other and the one where they share their experiences of the impact the illness has had on the group members' lives. This review is necessary if the new family is to be properly assimilated and to make sure they share the same knowledge base as the rest of the group.

Since the multifamily model is concerned with creating confidence and positive relationships, this induction for the new family supports the process. In the multifamily groups patients and relatives meet together, and the group leader tries to involve as many as possible of the family members who are close to the patient. Each meeting lasts for 90 minutes.

After the first two multifamily group meetings, the meeting structure is as follows:

15 min   Informal chat
20 min   'Round' (roundtable talk)
5 min   Selection of problem
45 min   Problem solving
5 min   Informal chat

The basic purpose of the group structure is to impart to participants a sense of confidence. This ensures that group members have a clear picture of what to expect in the groups. The structure also ensures that all group members are given an opportunity to participate actively.

The main elements in the psychoeducational multifamily groups are *problem solving*, *communication* and *education*. Since we have established a stable structure, the participants will feel secure enough to address practical issues in the problem-solving process. If secure boundaries and relationships are to be established, then *safety* and *predictability* are important elements in the life of the groups. This applies equally to the creation of a sense of *order* and *practical orientation* in the groups.

About 2 weeks after the educational seminar the multifamily group is launched. By that time the practical arrangements need to be set in place:

1   choice of day and time
2   location
3   layout of the room
4   provision of required equipment
5   refreshments.

Choice of day and time

Since the group will last for 2 years, we try to choose a day of the week that would suit most of the participants. The meetings should be held in the afternoon or evening to make sure that as many of the participants can attend as possible, irrespective of working hours or school times. It may prove difficult for relatives to get time off from work for such a long period. The relatives also need time for their evening meal, so 6.00–7.30 pm has proved to be a popular time since there is still some of the evening left at the end of the group meeting.

Location

A room capable of seating about 20 people is desirable. The interior should be light, simple and welcoming.

Layout of the room

If the chairs are arranged in a circle, this will offer both group leaders and members a clear view of all participants. A small table in the centre may be a useful place for the tea or coffee.

Provision of required equipment

The following equipment is required for group meetings: a white board, felt-tip pens, board cleaner, and a flipchart are very useful when the group is dealing with problem solving. One of the group leaders will write down the suggestions on the board. Felt-tip pens of different colours make it easier to capture the many ideas generated; a flipchart enables action plans to be clearly set down.

Refreshments

Usually coffee/tea and juice are served at group meetings. A friendly climate can develop when group members share a cup of coffee with other participants. It may also provide a safe focus when anxiety or the need for a cigarette becomes urgent. There are different views on the desirability of serving coffee at the meetings: for example, we are aware that caffeinated coffee is not served at multifamily groups in the USA because it is believed to increase anxiety.

It is important for group leaders to stick to the timetable. Some families may have difficulties in making the meetings; they may have babysitters at home or appointments after the group meetings. Often an hour and a half is enough for the patient, and they need to know that this time limit will not be exceeded.

The first multifamily group meeting
Anne Lise Øxnevad

After the educational seminar all members of the multifamily group, including patients, have a further meeting. The group leaders make sure that all the necessary equipment is in the room by then and arrange for coffee/tea and juice. The purpose of this group meeting is to help the participants become acquainted with one another.

When people come together in a group for the first time, they may be anxious to show their best qualities and are usually concerned with creating a positive atmosphere. The group leader explains that this meeting is to help them get to know one another and that when they next meet they will be able to talk about the illness and its impact. The group leader then explains that in order to get to know one another they could share accounts of their lives and work, their hobbies, their *likes and dislikes*, *where they like to go on holiday*, *what they do at weekends* etc. The group leader should start this round of contributions to act as a model for the group. Through such personal disclosure, the group leader is able to acknowledge membership of the group, in addition to leadership and facilitation roles.

An example of the first multifamily group meeting

Four families are introduced here. Some of them will be referred to later in the book.

The Browns: Peter, a patient, and his mother, Eva
The Whites: Karen, a patient, and her parents, Mary and Tom
The Blacks: [Maria, a patient who is still in hospital] Her parents, Ingrid and Allen
The Greens: James, a patient, his parents, Sam and George, and his sister Lilly

The group leader starts by saying: 'As you all know, my name is Anne Nelson. I am 44 years old. I work as a psychiatric nurse and have been working at this hospital for the last 12 years. I am married and have three children, all boys. Peter 18 years old, Hans 17 years old and Paul is 15. The eldest two go to high school, the youngest attends comprehensive school. My husband is a teacher and my youngest boy wants to become a teacher, too. The whole family is very fond of nature and we often go for walks in the forest and in the countryside. In my spare time I enjoy gardening — preferably plants and flowers. I'm useless at growing vegetables! I enjoy cooking, I often try new dishes, although the children don't always appreciate that!. At the moment we are redecorating the bathroom, which is taking its time.'

The group leader finishes by turning to the person sitting next. This is Eva Brown.

Eva Brown: Yes, my name is Eva Brown, I am Peter's mother. I am 42 and I lived alone with Peter until he moved into his own apartment two years ago. I live at Bainmoor, which is close to the sea. My house is old; my parents used to live there. The garden is big, but I enjoy working in it. I am a dentist and work at a school dental clinic. Peter and I have always managed well on our own and I have had good support from my siblings. We often spend time with them on weekends. I also attend a reading circle. This has become more difficult since Peter became ill. We've also got two dogs that need to be taken care of and walked.

Peter Brown: Yes, I am the son of the woman sitting next to me, and I am 22 years old. I only had six months of my engineering apprenticeship left when I became ill. I hope I will complete my education though. I've got two friends but I'm afraid they're getting tired of me, as I'm not up to very much these days. I used to play football, but I am not up to that either. Still, I watch all the football matches shown on TV. I also enjoy other things. I used to like playing computer games, but now I have problems concentrating, but I hope I am getting better. Now I'd rather have a sleep. I moved to my own flat two years ago. I thought it was very noisy and I felt unsure about the neighbours. I felt that they were spying on me.

Mary White: I am the mother of Karen and I'm 58 years old. I receive disability benefit, after working for many years as a cleaner. We live in a block of flats in Vinter. I enjoy needlework and I make national costumes. Every other week I meet my friends and we do our needlework together. In the evenings I watch TV, preferably nature programmes and crime serials. We've got two grandchildren who live in another part of the country and it is always nice when they come to see us. I am also in a community housing project, where I work as a cashier.

Karen White: I am 26 years old and work in a nursery, but right now I'm on sick leave. I don't really want to go back there as it had been so difficult before I got ill. I don't have any education, but I've always wanted to become a primary school teacher. Maybe I can do that later. I don't know what more to say.

Group leader: That's fine Karen, we will get better acquainted later. Let's talk to your father now.

Tom White: Well, I'm Karen's father. I'm 62, so Karen may think she's got an old dad. But I feel active and still work as a carpenter. In my spare time I like to do wood engraving and I have got my own workshop. My wife thinks there is too much woodwork in the house. Karen tried it also and the two of us have made a wall clock together. But since she got ill, we haven't done any work together. I also enjoy fishing and some weekends I go fishing with my brother-in-law. But at the moment my prime concern is Karen getting well and I hope we'll get help from the group.

Group leader: That's nice to hear.

Then she presents the other group leader who introduces herself.

Ingrid Black: I'm Maria's mother, and she is still in hospital. Looks like it's going to take some time. I am 40 years old, I am a teacher, but I work half-time, as a special needs teacher. That's quite enough as Maria's illness is tiring. We also have two younger children. Maria is the eldest, she is 17; there is also Nina who is 14, and Rory, 10. I have been an active member of the National Union of Teachers, but at present that's too much for me. We live at Gander and have a house with a garden. Allen looks after the garden. We have a cabin in the mountains and enjoy walking there. I also have to take care of my old, sick mother, so I feel quite exhausted. The best way for me to relax is to listen to music. Sometimes I try to get to concerts.

Allen Black: As you know, I am Ingrid's husband and Maria's father. I think it's sad that Maria's not here. I'm 49 years old and I'm an economist working for an oil company. I enjoy my work, even though there are periods with a lot of overtime, which puts a lot of responsibility and work on my wife, too. But I do all the gardening, so she doesn't have to worry about that. I can relax when I'm working in the garden and I enjoy watching plants grow and sprout. I like to try out new things, especially with roses and rare plants and I'm very proud when I succeed. I try to keep in shape and jog before going to work in the morning. I'm also worried about our daughter Maria and I find what we go through with her scary and exhausting. Thank you.

Samantha Green: I'm James's mother and I'm 51 years old. I work at a bookstore, part-time for about 30 hours a week. We live in a semi-detached house in Carsham and have been living there ever since we got married. I enjoy living close to the centre. In my spare time I enjoy reading and I guess that's why I enjoy my work so much. Once a week I work out at the gym and I also enjoy taking walks. Sometimes during the weekend my husband and I go to old-time dancing, but this has been difficult since James has become ill.

Lilly Berger: I am James's sister, I'm 27. I live in a flat in my parents' basement and I am a single mother of Mervin who is 7 now. In nine months' time I'll have finished my nursing studies and I'm looking forward to earning some money. James and I have always been good friends and he used to help me a lot with babysitting before he became ill and started drinking. So, I would like to help him. Now that I am a student I don't have much spare time, but at weekends Mervin stays with his father and I try to keep in contact with my friends. I also try to do a bit of photography. James likes that as well and in the past we used to go on hiking tours together and took many nice nature pictures. Right now I'm most concerned with James getting better, as his drinking causes a lot of rows at home.

George Green: Well, I am James's father or stepfather to be exact. I am 50 years old and work as a plumber, I run my own business. Samantha and I married when James was 14. James's father had been killed in a car accident three years before that. So things haven't always been easy for James. As my wife said we enjoy old-time dancing and we hope that James will get better so that we can continue with that. I also enjoy fishing and I have an old boat I sometimes go fishing in. Well, I think that's about it.

James Green: I'm 18 years old and I'm an apprentice plumber. However, since I became ill I have been off for three months. I don't really want to be in this group, but I'll see what happens. I think they are exaggerating when they talk about my drinking. I was working at getting my driving licence when I became ill and I hope I'll soon be well enough to take it up again. What I like best is to stay in my room and listen to music. My sister wants me to go walking with her, but I'm not up to it.

The group members usually follow the model of the group leaders, but occasionally family members might start talking for others rather than for themselves or talk too much about the illness. The group leader would then interrupt them saying: 'This time we'd like to hear a bit more about you,' or 'It's understandable for you to want to talk about the illness, but let's save that for the next meeting.'

Some group members find it too difficult to talk about themselves. If that happens, the group leader might ask for more details to help them get started. If someone, for example, tells us that they enjoy music and then falls silent, the group leader could ask what kind of music they prefer.

Sometimes group members are very insecure and have problems talking about themselves even if the group leaders help them get started. In such cases, the group leader should emphasize the benefits of getting to know others and stress that it usually gets easier to talk after some time in the group. Disclosing such information about themselves is important as it will enable relationships to be formed across the families on the basis of shared interests. This information will also be useful for the later network building.

Here the group members meet as ordinary people, and the focus is on the resources the families possess. Some families lead a socially withdrawn life and the illness takes up most of their time. The group may, in this respect, serve as a source of help in maintaining social competence and the patients' participation in it may be regarded as social skills training.

Before the group meeting ends the group leader summarizes the information the group members have contributed. Already at this stage we try to encourage relationships between group members. These relationships could be based on common interests, similar family structure, comparable occupations etc.

The group meeting is closed by the group leader who thanks the group members for coming and reminds them about the next meeting.

The second multifamily group meeting
Anne Lise Øxnevad

During the second multifamily group meeting members disclose how the illness has affected their lives. Just as at the initial meeting, they are likely to be influenced by the group leader's example. McFarlane's findings suggest that it is important for group leaders to share as much as possible in both professional and personal domains. From the professional point of view, for example, group leaders might recount how they became interested in this field and the way they feel when treating the illness, including feelings of frustration as well as success. From a personal point of view, group leaders might talk about their family members, friends or patients they have been close to. It is important for them to set an example and reveal their feelings in relation to experiences which families are often reluctant to divulge.

After the initial welcome, the group leader refers to the whiteboard, drawing everybody's attention to the agenda: *15 minutes of informal conversation, 70 minutes of roundtable discussion and, finally, 5 more minutes of conversation.*

The group leader continues by saying: 'I'm happy to see everyone here again. At the last meeting we got to know each other and today we will begin by chatting for 15 minutes – we could even continue from where we stopped last time. Afterwards we are going on to talk about how the illness has affected our lives.' The group leader begins the conversation, for example, by saying: 'Last weekend I went for a hike in the Lake District. Has anyone else been there?'

From the second meeting on, all multifamily group meetings begin with a social conversation or chat. The purpose of this is to create an atmosphere of ease in the group, a system of mutual social support. This can be achieved by group leaders showing genuine interest in each of the group members and also by drawing attention to interests that might be common to group members. This social conversation of 15 minutes should not involve any discussion of mental illness. Here, the group leaders are acting as colleagues, on a par with the group members, and not as therapists. The relationship should be equal and fraternal. This will strengthen group members' sense of their own competence and power to tackle their problems. Furthermore, it offers group members the chance of developing personal relationships and of establishing a social support system.

McFarlane believes that the family needs such a support system to deal with the confusion, anxiety and exhaustion its members may experience. In the social conversation, the group leaders model how to establish that kind of conversation in the group.

After 15 minutes of chatting, the group leader may say:

As I have already told you today we will talk about how the illness has affected our lives. I will start by talking about my own experiences. I wonder whether my choice of current occupation was influenced by the fact that someone in my family suffered from a serious mental illness.

As far as I can remember my uncle had a chronic mental illness. He was shy and withdrawn and was hospitalized several times. This was very hard for my grandmother as he lived with her and she was the one who had to care for him all through his long illness. Gradually this affected the entire family because during holidays and social events we had to take responsibility as well. My uncle was alone; he had no friends and was not able to stay with us if there were other people there. I remember feeling embarrassed but also frightened, too. When he didn't answer my questions I would become angry. Later I realized why my uncle was like that and why our family had to put up with it.

The feeling of what the illness brings to the family can be common to all of us: anxiety, fear, confusion, uncertainty, shame, guilt, anger, sadness, grief and frustration. I remember my first experience at the hospital when I started working as a nurse and I was to look after a psychotic man. I was actually scared and anxious about the symptoms he had but, during a meeting with him, I saw that he was even more frightened than I and needed my help both as a professional and as a fellow human being. As I acquired more knowledge about treating psychosis, both through theory and practice, I became more secure when dealing with psychotic patients.

James' stepfather: Yes, I'm James' stepfather, and I have noticed that our relationship has become worse since James got ill. I become sad and sorry every time he isn't well and I worry about his drinking at weekends. When I talk to him he becomes angry and says it's none of my business because I'm not his father. I also found it hard when he was hospitalized because he felt that it was me who had arranged for his forced admission. It is a bit disappointing that we cannot go to old-time dancing since we have to look after James during the weekends. But I hope we will get some help here because I want to support James just as if he were my own son.

The conversation goes around half of the circle, then the other group leader speaks after which the rest of the group continue.

Some will find it difficult to talk about their experiences; for some it may be hard to find the right words to explain their ordeal; while others may struggle with their feelings.

It is important that everyone should have time and space to say something, and that the group leader should help everyone to get started, for example, by asking questions like: 'Will you be able to go on holiday this year?' Or: 'Is there anything that has become more difficult for the family since James got ill?'

The group leader explains that it is up to everyone to decide how much or how little they should reveal.

When all the group members have finished, the group leader thanks them for their contributions and may also add: 'Do you recognize what's being described? Many of you may have had similar experiences.' This gives the families a sense of community and they discover that they are not alone in having such experiences, thoughts and feelings about an ill family member.

The patients also contribute to these rounds. The feeling of community is important both to the family members and to the patient. For some families it might be the first time they have heard their ill son or daughter talk about their own experience, which might include feelings of guilt because of the suffering they have caused to the family, loss of friends, fear of another psychotic episode, the parents' taking control of their lives and so on.

This meeting is often characterized by a sense of grief, sadness, anger and frustration. But we know from experience that it is also full of positive feelings. Family members and patients provide each other with sound support and care through the sense of community that they achieve when identifying with each others' experiences. To share each other's pain creates a feeling of community and a secure atmosphere in the group.

It is important for the group leader to be sympathetic and to show understanding of the situation at the same time as directing the group. Sometimes the families are very eager and may present some well-defined problems that they want to be resolved during the meeting. The group leader should respond by saying that it is good that the problems have been touched on and that these are just some of the problems they will be working on together when they start problem solving during the next meeting. And then the group leader asks the group members to raise the question again, at the next meeting.

In some groups time is too short to hear what all members have to say during the roundtable talk and so we continue the round in the next meeting. At the end of the meeting the last 5 minutes are spent chatting.

Social conversation (chat)

The social conversation is a very important part of the work in family groups. We use this both when we have individual conversations with each family and when working in a group. The only exception is the first time the group meets, when the group members introduce themselves. In the group, the social conversation lasts for 15 minutes. During individual meetings, it has proved better if less time is spent on this kind of activity. The social conversation starts on time regardless of any latecomers. In this conversation we often talk about everyday events which could be easily shared with people one does not know very well. The group leaders show interest in the events in group members' lives that do not concern illness. If necessary one of the group leaders will take the initiative by introducing a subject for conversation. The content of the conversation is kept 'light'. The group leader, being a model, sets an appropriate tone for the conversation in line with the chosen subject. They ask questions and help the conversation along. Examples of good conversational topics can be holidays, weather, food, children, hobbies, films, sports, TV or local events. At this stage any complaints or criticism about the patients are diverted, ignored or reformulated. The group leader points to the next phase by saying something like: 'We would like to hear more about this, so we'll come back to it during the roundtable talk when we'll have a closer look at the problem.'

The group leader tries to share contributions among the group members to ensure that everyone has a chance to talk during the social conversation. Everyone is encouraged to take part, but no one should be pressurized into contributing to the conversation if they find it too uncomfortable. The group leaders also make sure that no one group member dominates the conversation. The participants are told to talk directly to each other and are encouraged to stick to socially acceptable behaviour.

The group leaders should intervene whenever several people are speaking at once. They should also ensure that they are not drawn into such conversations by saying, for example: 'Excuse me, I would really love to hear what you all have to say, but I can only listen to one person at a time.'

The group leaders also need to set limits on interruptions and 'talking on behalf of others' by saying, for example: 'Please keep that in mind and we'll get back to it later.' Or, 'John, your father says that you are OK with this, has he understood you correctly?'

The social conversation serves to underline the equality of relationship between the patients, family members and the group leaders. The group members' resources may become evident here. It is useful to focus on day-to-day events to demonstrate that not everything in life centres around the illness. This enables the participants to make contacts not only in relation to the illness but through common interests as well. The families tend to become very interested in each other. This sequence is important in creating a sense of community. The family members have a place they belong to, where they can find support in case things become difficult.

To be a relative of a person suffering from a serious mental illness also involves social withdrawal and reduced social activity in comparison to the pre-onset situation. This is partly due to the difficulty relatives may experience in focusing on subjects outside of the dominating illness.

The significant burden of being a carer in such circumstances may lead to social withdrawal, since the patient may not be able to tolerate social situations or may behave inappropriately. Thus, for the patient, isolation may be a social effect of the illness. As a consequence of this isolation, the patient's social skills are often reduced. The social conversation in the group can offer patients the chance of practising their social skills and may help maintain such competence during this difficult period. Another important factor is the lightening of atmosphere in the group when patients are able to participate in conversation, and this can ease the transition to a successful problem-solving session.

After 15 minutes social conversation it is time to move on. The group leader makes this explicit when they start the 'roundtable talk', saying, for example: 'Now it's time for the round. This is where we'll be discussing problems related to the illness.'

Problem solving
Trond Grønnestad

During the previous group meeting the participants have talked about how having an ill family member has affected them. After 15 minutes of social chatting the group has 20 minutes at its disposal for the so-called 'go-round'. We call it the 'go-round' because each group member is given time to talk, in succession, and the participants sit in a circle. Now we will move on to the problem-solving phase, where the timetable is as follows:

15 min   Informal chat
20 min   'Go-round' (roundtable talk)
 5 min   Selection of problem
45 min   Problem solving
 5 min   Informal chat

We will now take a closer look at the structured conversation around the table (in a circle), where the families talk one after another about their problems, including their management of the problems). The 15 minutes of chatting are followed by the go-round which takes 20 minutes. The round has two purposes: to elicit families' concerns and dilemmas in regard to the illness and, using this information, to choose a problem to work on during the problem-solving part of the session. This 20 minutes' go-round should be divided up so that all families become involved. The group leader starts the round by asking the family, whose problem had been addressed at the previous meeting, how it went and if the solution worked.

The group leader needs to be positive and accommodating and to offer support to the patient and family whose problem is being addressed. Where the problem solving has proved ineffective or unsuccessful, the group leader looks in detail with the family at any factors that may have been ignored; for example if the family members had rushed the process or skipped some of the details when implementing the suggested solution. The group leader assumes responsibility for this outcome so that the family or patient do not feel failures.

After this, the round continues. The group leader first addresses the patient of the family whose turn it is to present. This is to underline the fact that the patient is the principal character. The patient is addressed by name, as, for instance: 'Peter, have you had any difficulties since our last meeting?'

It is important to ask the questions in the right way. If we just ask 'how have things been since the last meeting?', it may prove more difficult to identify problematic areas. It may also prove difficult to keep track of time during the session, and the co-leader should help here.

The group leaders should always keep in mind the warning signs of relapse and if a patient does show such a sign, it should be noted at once. In identifying such problems, it will be noted that some have a higher order of significance:

1   *Warning signs of relapse*:
    Example: James' mother has noticed that James has been more irritable the last few days. He looks anxious and sometimes wanders around at night. These symptoms are identical to the ones he had prior to the onset of the illness and these have been identified as warning signs.
2   *Safety at home*: (aggressive behaviour, smoking in bed, etc.)
    Example: Maria stayed at home on a day's leave. At the time the family had some visitors with small children. The children were quite noisy and Maria became more and more restless and vocal. The situation deteriorated until finally Maria lost control and hit a 1-year-old child, yelling at him and being verbally aggressive. This posed a problem for the parents. They were apprehensive about Maria's future home visits and were frightened that she would become violent towards her younger siblings.
3   *Medication*:
    Example: Karen wants to stop taking her medication because she gains weight. James wants to stop his medication to be able to drink alcohol at weekends.
4   *Drugs/alcohol*:
    Example: James started drinking quite a lot of alcohol at weekends and his parents think his condition is worsening.
5   *Family events, celebrations, deaths, etc.*:
    Example: It is Maria's father's 50th birthday, and the family are going to have a big party. Everyone expects Maria to take a day's leave to be there, but she refuses; it ends in conflict within the family, which is stressful for the patient.

6   *Change in treatment (for instance change of therapist)*:
Example: Peter's therapist is leaving and Peter becomes anxious and withdrawn.
7   *Economic problems*:
Example: Karen took out a big mortgage to buy her apartment and now has difficulties paying it off following her illness.
8   *Discord within the family*:
Example: Peter's mother is worried about her son's sleeping habits. She is annoyed that his condition has not improved and it results in a conflict between mother and son.
9   *Deviations from the guidelines given at the educational seminar*: (for instance, the family demand too much of the patient, rush things etc.)
Example: James' stepfather wants him to resume his work as an apprentice plumber as soon as he is discharged from hospital. He thinks that work is the best medicine. But James is unable to get back to work.

In the roundtable talk, when each family talks about what is difficult in the illness of their family member, a lot of emotions and statements may be difficult to handle. These can be anger, guilt, anxiety and so on. The group leader shows empathy and tries to reformulate everybody's statements in a positive way. Every opportunity to educate is used.

Some families become enthusiastically engaged in the activity, so they may start speaking all at once. This will often confuse the patient who may have difficulties concentrating. When this happens it is important for the group leader to resolve this in a positive way, by saying, for example: 'I can't hear what everyone is saying, could you please talk one at a time?'

It is also a good idea to write down the communication rules and put them on the wall as a reminder.

Example of a round:

Group leader: How have things been at home for the last two weeks, Peter?
Peter: I am very tired in the mornings. Mum is constantly nagging and wants me to get up earlier.
Group leader: How long has it been since you were discharged from hospital?
Peter: Four weeks. And I have increased the dosage of my medicine because of the voices. I need to sleep till 11.
Peter's mum: I think it's only fair that now that he's out of hospital he should have breakfast with me.
Group leader: Do you remember the educational seminar, when we talked about an increased need for sleep, in relation to both the psychosis and medication? It's normal to need more sleep, but at the same time it is important to have a good pattern of living; that is to go to bed as usual

at night. I can understand parents wanting a speedy recovery and to a return to the old routine, but it is important to be patient, to take one step at a time.

Peter's mum: I guess I have to lower my expectations and be more patient.

Group leader: How have you been Karen?

Karen: I wish I didn't have to take my medication. I get so thirsty and my throat becomes really parched.

Karen's mum: She drinks gallons of Coca-cola and she's putting on a lot of weight.

Group leader: It's important that you take your medicine, Karen, to prevent a relapse. You could try drinking sugar-free soda or water instead.

Karen's father: I have suggested trying sugar-free sweets or chewing gum, which she's agreed to try.

Group leader: That's good, Karen. Next time you could tell us how you're doing.

Group leader: Mr and Mrs Black, as far as I understand, Maria is still in hospital.

Maria's mum: Yes, we feel that she's worse than ever, and we worry about her two younger siblings at home who have lots of concerns and seem anxious.

Group leader: I can well understand your anxieties, in relation to Maria and to your other two children. It must be very hard for you. Do you think we could find some time after the meeting to arrange an appointment for me to come to your place and we could talk together, all of us?

Mr Black: We would like that very much.

Group leader: James, how have things been for the last couple of weeks? Have there been any problems?

(James, his parents and sister all talk at once, his father is rather angry.)

Group leader: I can't understand what you're saying when you all talk at the same time. Let's start with you, James.

James: There are a lot of quarrels at home about alcohol. But I think they exaggerate things.

Group leader: What do you think about alcohol, James, what do you think is reasonable?

James: I should be allowed to have a couple of beers over the weekends.

James' father: We feel that James is worse now that he's drinking alcohol at the weekend.

Group leader: In what way is he worse?

James' mum: He's more irritable and seems anxious. He has sleeping problems, wanders around a bit at night. I'm afraid he will relapse.

Group leader: How are you feeling James; is it the way your parents describe?

James: I guess so and what you said earlier about medicine and alcohol not going together might be true, but then I'd rather stop taking my medicine.

James' sister, Lilly: Do you remember, James, how good things were when you didn't touch a drop?

The 20 minutes' round is over, and all families have participated in turn. The next 5 minutes are given over to choosing a problem to be solved at this meeting. This is always the group leader's choice.

Choosing a problem for problem solving

The round is finished by thanking all the families for participating. The group leaders then turn to each other and discuss between themselves which problem should be resolved this time. They talk out loud so that the group members can hear what they are saying. They have 5 minutes to make their final choice.

We want as many families as possible to have their problem resolved (rotation every six meetings). The families that will not have their problem resolved this time will find it useful to listen to the way others' problems have been resolved, since they may well have had or may still have similar problems. As mentioned earlier, there are two main things the group leaders should be aware of:

1   factors that may cause relapse
2   themes concerning the next stage in the treatment.

Furthermore, it is important to take into consideration possible deterioration of symptoms. The following are of special importance:

- Safety at home, for instance smoking in bed, aggressive behaviour.
- Family collaboration over the taking of medicine.
- Drugs and alcohol.
- Events within the family, such as family gatherings, moving home, loss of a close family member etc.
- Events outside the family, like change of therapist, change in social support etc.
- Disagreement within the family.
- 'Conflicts' with the guidelines received at the seminar day (moving too fast, too high expectations etc.).

When several problems are presented, the group leaders should use their own judgement to choose the right problem for the session. To this end, the group leader asks detailed questions, such as 'How long has the problem existed?'; 'What's been tried earlier?'; 'What were the consequences of similar situations?'; and finally 'How urgent is the problem?'

If the group leader decides not to work on a particular problem there are several possibilities:

1 To offer a solution to the problem and then, at the next meeting, ask the family to report back on how it worked.
2 If it is a crisis, to offer a meeting outside the group.
3 To refer to an earlier solution of the same problem and ask the family to try it.

If there are new families in the group, they should be spared problem solving during their first meeting. The group leader must always keep in mind the specific stage of treatment the patient has reached. As time goes by the group leader will notice that the focus of attention changes from problems connected with worsening symptoms to problems related to the next step in the process of recovery.

Problem solving

Problem solving can be roughly divided into three stages:

1 mapping the problem
2 suggesting solutions
3 evaluation.

The problem can be a situation, a person or a group. If a solution is to be found, the problem must be within an area the family can control.

Problems presented can be of three different categories:

- Mismatch between the desired state and reality. For instance, where the patient cannot handle a given task (e.g. to go to school).
- Problems in developing a task. For instance, how to modify a goal in order to improve functioning (in order to gain knowledge).
- Speculations; for instance, brooding over possible difficulties that *might* occur (What if I don't tolerate the medication?)

Here we will concentrate on the 'mismatch' category as this kind of problem is prevalent in problem-solving work with families. **NB** When we choose a mismatch problem for resolution we should choose one that presents a reasonable chance of success before we try to tackle the most difficult and most complex situations.

Mapping the problem

The process of problem solving starts with a close scrutiny of the problem to throw light on it as far as we can. Before one can start the solving of a mismatch, it is important to be aware of the norm. The problem should be described as precisely as possible and we need to ascertain who is involved, where, when, in what way and so on. The causes of the mismatch should be mapped in the most careful way possible.

When investigating a problem situation, it is also necessary to state the goals of each of the family members. The group leaders should here try to define the problem in a way that might lead to a solution. All family members should acknowledge and support the definition.

The definition of the problem should be short and concise, but provide enough information to give the participants a general view of what it is all about. Another option is to ask family members what it would take to eliminate the mismatch and reach the goal.

In the following example, Dad is celebrating his 50th birthday. Family and friends have gathered together in a hotel nearby. Maria doesn't want to disappoint her father, but says she daren't come to the party. This causes a conflict at home. Dad doesn't want to have a party without Maria. When investigating the problem, it turns out that everyone wants to have a party, including Maria, but she doesn't know how to participate. As everyone agrees on the goal – that Dad should have his party – the problem can be described in terms of that goal.

> Thus the definition of the problem is:
> *How can Maria manage to go to her father's birthday party?*
> The alternative is to describe the situation:
> *It is her father's 50th birthday. Maria wishes to go to the party, but doesn't know how to do it.*

The problem here is related to the situation: her father's 50th birthday. When defining the problem it is important to attach the problem to the situation causing the problem and not to any particular person. If a person is defined as the problem, that person will be offended and there will be no problem solving.

Suggesting solutions

The next step in the problem-solving method is to find a solution to the problem. This process is called *brainstorming*. Here we ask all the group members to suggest solutions. The principle here is that all suggestions are good suggestions. Suggestions cannot be evaluated at this stage as this will 'kill' or destroy the brainstorming. All the suggestions are gratefully accepted and written on the board.

There are four main principles in the brainstorming:

1   No negative criticism.
2   All ideas are good, no matter how 'wild' they seem.
3   Quantity leads to quality.
4   When the total number of ideas increases, so does the number of valuable ideas.

Evaluation

The last stage in the process of problem solving is *evaluation*. Here the suggestions from the brainstorming are evaluated. Both advantages and disadvantages of each of the suggestions are discussed. And while doing so one can ask if a given suggestion might lead to the solving of the problem. This is a good way to filter out the 'solutions' that will not lead to the elimination of the problem, so that there is no need to spend time assessing them (Anderson *et al.* 1986). In family work, we use the general problem-solving technique of the brainstorming method as described earlier. Further, we use a structured approach, and here it is important to remember:

- Go slowly.
- Remain emotionally calm.
- Set limits.
- Keep it simple.
- Solve the problem step by step.

When you are in the middle of the process of problem solving, you may often be too emotionally involved to find a constructive solution. Falloon *et al.* (1984) say:

> Some families never structure family discussions, and in other families the efforts to conduct a discussion escalate into emotional exchanges that merely raise everybody's tension without leading to any effective resolving of the problem. For these reasons, we have found it extremely helpful to train families to utilise a structured problem solving method to facilitate their coping efforts.

By using a structured problem-solving method we can make the problem easy to understand for everyone in the group and, at the same time, possible to resolve. When the problem is accessible to all the group members they will contribute their previous experience. Thus we receive more suggestions for solutions than we would if the family tried to resolve the problem alone. This gives hope that some change is possible.

To recap: we divide the problem-solving process into seven steps:

1   *Defining the problem*:
    What is the problem in this situation? Talk about the problem. Listen carefully to what is said and ask questions. Try to get all the family members' opinion on the problem. Then write down the exact definition of the problem.

    _____

2   *Make up a list of possible solutions – brainstorming*:
    Here all group members should make their suggestions. All suggestions are good. No criticism is allowed at this point. Assessment or criticism at this stage will inhibit the creativity of the brainstorming. Write down all the proposals.
    1 _____
    2 _____
    3 _____
    4 _____
    5 _____
    6 _____

3   *Assessment of the advantages and disadvantages of each suggestion*:
    The question can be asked: 'Will this suggestion lead to a resolution of the problem, and are there any suggestions the family would like to have a closer look at?'
        If the suggestion cannot lead to a resolution, or if the family does not want to work with it, it is crossed off list.

4   *Choosing a solution*:
    It is the family that chooses the solution they want to try, or possibly a combination of several solutions.

    _____

5   *What resources are necessary to resolve the problem?*
    'Resources' means those things that are required to carry out the solution. It can be time, courage, patience, money, effort etc.
6   *Decide on a particular time and place for carrying out the solution.*
7   *Go through the plan and commend everyone for their participation.*

   The evaluation of the problem-solving project takes place at the next group meeting. During the roundtable talk, the family whose problem was discussed at the previous meeting is asked if they have tried the suggestion. If the family have succeeded, they are given credit for their efforts. If the suggestion did not lead to a resolution of the problem then the group leader takes the blame. There can be several reasons why the family did not manage to implement the suggestion:

- The problem was too pervasive.
- The process of solving the problem is at a very early stage.
- The group leaders were too eager to find a solution and forgot to take the family into consideration.
- The group leaders did not investigate the problem/mismatch as thoroughly as they should have done it.
- Other factors.

The main point here is that the family should not experience a further failure.

Table 2.2 illustrates what the whiteboard may look like after problem solving.

The family chose a combination of several suggestions: Maria would be seated at the end of the table, close to the door and next to her cousin, whom she knew well.

It is important to keep the board tidy. By using many colours, it is easier to distinguish between the various suggestions.

Table 2.2 Problem solving on a whiteboard

Definition, problem		
How should Maria manage to attend her fathers 50th birthday?		
Suggestions	Advantages	Disadvantages
Sit next to someone she knows	Will feel secure	
Sit at the end of the table, close to the door, so that she can leave whenever she wants to	There will be someone to talk to Will feel safer	Others may wonder why she is leaving
Have a separate room where Maria could go in case she wants to withdraw from the event	Feels safer	Costly May be tempting to just stay in the room
Not go to the party	Will not have to be anxious	Does not solve the problem
Say that she has got the flu		This will disappoint her Dad
Mum should tell the guests not to ask Maria how she is doing	Does not have to worry about 'uncomfortable' questions	There is no need to let everyone know that Maria has got a mental illness

Crisis intervention plan
Trond Grønnestad

It is important to offer each patient and his/her family help to work out an emergency plan. This is a detailed plan showing what the patient and family should do if and when the patient should deteriorate. The emergency plan is a means of preventing relapse. The plan is based on the patient's warning signs of relapse. The patient, together with the family, develops a language that others can understand. Statements like: 'John is not doing so well' and 'John is much worse now' do not tell us much. The family do not have anything to compare with and thus the statements are merely subjective assumptions, which can easily lead to arguments and quarrels between the patient and his family on the one side and the hospital on the other. In Smeby's study, described earlier, 36% of patients had asked the health services for help, but were turned away. Later, they were admitted compulsorily.

If we look out for warning signs, we could say instead: 'John has been up a lot during the night; he seems more irritable than usual and stays in his room. It looks like he is showing warning signs of relapse.'

When the patient shows such signs it is important to initiate action, which may include lowering stress factors or increasing protection factors or both. When making up an emergency plan, we ask the patient to make a note of the three or four most usual warning signs – the ones the patient is certain he/she has and which are most noticeable. These signals are put down under point 1: My warning signals of relapse are . . .

Going about creating a plan

The emergency plan is meant to prevent relapse and can be used by both the family and the patient (see Figure 2.3). The plan is made by the patient together with his/her family and group leader.

The group leader asks the family if they agree that these warning signs are the most characteristic ones. The following example illustrates such a situation:

Group leader: John, I can see that you have chosen sleeping problems, concentration problems and lack of interest in doing things as your most common warning signs. Do you [parents] agree that these are John's most typical warning signs?
Dad: I agree that he has problems with his sleep, but what I notice most is that he gets annoyed by some trifles and isolates himself in his room.
Group leader: Do you agree with this, John?
John: It's quite possible that my Dad notices different things than me, but I first notice the warning signs I've already mentioned.
Group leader: You notice warning signs from different perspectives. You,

---

1 Go through the recorded warning signs

My warning signs are:

a _____

b _____

c _____

d _____

e _____

Efforts:

_____

_____

_____

2 If this does not help, get in touch with your contact person who will, in agreement with you, decide whether your therapist should be contacted

Contact person _____

Telephone no. _____

3 If your contact person is not available at the moment, get in touch with your therapist to get help

Therapist _____

Telephone no. _____

4 If your therapist is not available, get in touch with the emergency services/department

Telephone no. _____

5 Contact person's signature _____

Patient's signature _____

A copy of this emergency plan is given to the patient and the family and one copy is put into the medical records/case history

---

Figure 2.3 Example emergency plan.

John, feel them physically, but the rest of the family will see later what John is already feeling. Do you think we could agree to write down John's three warning signs and add one of the warning signals that Dad noticed? What do you think about that, John?

To avoid getting into uncomfortable discussions about John's warning signals, the group leader takes control of the situation. The group leader must be on the alert so that none of the parties feels offended. In this example, the patient included all of his warning signs of relapse, but he had to accept that the warning sign his Dad noticed had to be included too.

The next step in the emergency plan is to find out about the family's own strategies for avoiding relapse. Most patients and family members have their own methods to deal with the symptoms and the problems the illness causes. However, not all of them are aware that they do have such coping strategies. They act without thinking these over beforehand. While they are often good and effective efforts, they can often have the exactly opposite result.

The level of stress and anxiety in the family is often decisive in what strategies they use. When families realize that what they do to handle the symptoms does not have the expected effect, they soon find themselves in a situation of 'not managing'. This is a situation which leads to stress reactions and causes anxiety within the family. One definition of stress is: 'Not really managing'.

To deal with this difficulty the family will automatically try to gain control over the patient and the situation. This will turn the family into a high EE family, which, in turn, will increase the risk of relapse.

The following is an example of how the family can get help to find coping strategies:

Group leader: Now we have put down the warning signals: sleeping problems, lack of interest in doing things, concentration problems, and John getting annoyed by trivial matters. Some of these warning signs John notices first (lack of interest and concentration problems) while some are first noticed by the family (increased irritability). What we will do next is to find coping strategies for these warning signals. Let us first concentrate on the warning sign regarding sleep disturbances. Do you know anything that helps? Perhaps you have tried something?

John: I have tried to go to bed earlier, but that didn't help. Just can't lie still.

Mum: We notice it when he is up at nights, but I don't know if he has tried anything to change it.

Group leader: Let's take a look at the next warning sign – no interest in doing things. What do you do when you notice it?

John: When I get that warning sign, everything becomes stressful. I have no strategy to deal with this warning signal.

Dad: We haven't been aware that this is part of the illness. I know I get irritated when John is lazy, so I start hassling to get him going again. This often results in John locking himself up in his room.

Group leader: It's common for parents to get irritated with what we call 'negative symptoms'. These are symptoms like withdrawal, lack of initiative, etc. and they can make the patient seem lazy. Now let us look at the last two warning signs, I mean concentration problems and increased irritability. What do you do when you notice these signs?

Mum: We don't notice concentration problems much, but we do notice his increased irritability. When we do, we leave him alone. Sometimes this affects the rest of the family, but at least we avoid fights. We walk a bit on tiptoes because we don't want to provoke him too much since he's so irritable.

John: I don't have any way of managing these two warning signs. I think the only thing that could help regarding concentration problems is to keep to myself a bit. I get so tired when I am with others.

Group leader: It isn't easy to find effective measures for each of the warning signs. I notice that you, John, have found out that to spend some time alone helps regarding concentration problems. Then you [parents] let John have some time to himself when you notice that he is irritated. This is probably a good strategy for avoiding confrontation. At the same time there is the danger that the boundaries of what is acceptable are extended gradually. Have you noticed if there are special situations when John gets his warning signs? Has he, for instance, stopped taking his medicine, used any intoxicants, or are there things in the environment that stress him?

Dad: The last time John was hospitalized he had stopped taking his medicines. We didn't notice before it was too late.

John: I stopped taking medication because I got so stressed with all the hassle about having to go back to school, so I wasn't able to take my medicine because it made me feel dull.

Group leader: I see that there are two important lessons for you. One thing is that John needs to take it easy for some time yet. I think it's too early for John to resume his studies. The other thing is that John gets ill when he stops taking his medicine. When John shows warning signs of relapse there are some simple efforts you should make:

1 Ask John if he is taking his medicine.
2 Find out if there is anything stressing John.
3 John protects himself against things he finds stressful.
4 Avoid hassling John when he has warning signals.
NB Don't extend the limits of what is acceptable!
How does this sound to you? Do you think you could do this?

John: It is OK with me.

Dad: Seems so simple, but we still haven't been able to do it because none of us knew what to do and what was right. We never got in a position to talk about this.

The family members had little experience in dealing with John's warning signs. Therefore they were very uncertain as to which strategies would be effective. What became evident, however, was that John still had a low stress threshold. He also got ill when he stopped taking his medication. John found that it helped him with concentration problems to shield himself from stressful situations. In this example, his Dad thought that a characteristic warning sign of relapse was John's locking himself up in his room. It might be a warning sign, but in that situation it was just as much a coping strategy that John used for dealing with concentration problems. We would not have found this out if we had not explored the efforts or strategies related to a particular warning sign.

When exploring what may lead to warning signs of relapse, it may be useful to look at the model shown in Figure 2.4.

Point 2 in the emergency plan is to write down a contact person's name that will help monitor the warning signs. The contact person should be someone the patient knows well, trusts and meets regularly. In the case just described, John chose his parents to be contact persons. The contact person has two main tasks regarding the emergency plan:

1   Inform the patient when he notices that the patient has warning signs of relapse.
2   Help the patient manage the warning signs or help get in touch with the persons listed in the emergency plan.

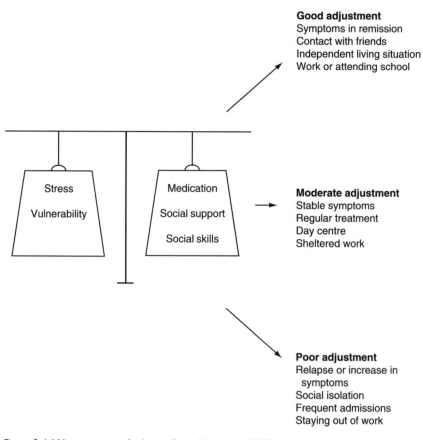

Good adjustment
Symptoms in remission
Contact with friends
Independent living situation
Work or attending school

Stress

Vulnerability

Medication

Social support

Social skills

Moderate adjustment
Stable symptoms
Regular treatment
Day centre
Sheltered work

Poor adjustment
Relapse or increase in
  symptoms
Social isolation
Frequent admissions
Staying out of work

Figure 2.4 Warning signs of relapse (from Liberman 1989).

In points 3 and 4, you put down the names and the telephone numbers of the people in the health services who can be of help if you cannot manage the warning signs by yourselves. Every patient has a therapist who has a copy of the emergency plan. Some also stay in contact with nursing staff in the hospital whom they can contact in difficult times. If the persons you know in the healthcare system are not available, call the emergency department. This telephone number should also be listed in the emergency plan.

Finally (point 5), both the patient and the contact person sign the emergency plan. An emergency plan like this works at different levels:

- The patient and the relatives know what the signs of relapse are, thus they can relax regarding other signs. Many patients have told us stories of how hard it is to have the parents or a spouse watch over them all the times. A female patient said that after she had been discharged from hospital she could never be herself when visiting friends: her husband kept pulling her up short every time she laughed.
- The family develop a shared language and they get to talk together about the things they observe. When formulating the emergency plan the group leader sets up a channel of communication so that the family, at a later stage, can talk about the specific warning signs.
- Last, but not least, the development of a language to talk about warning signs will contribute to getting help at an earlier stage. It is much easier to turn down a family that merely says that the patient has deteriorated than a family saying that they now observe these warning signs (sleeping problems, isolation and so on) and that these are indicators of relapse. In short, the emergency plan provides:

1 security
2 readiness
3 early help.

A family from one of the groups was asked how the summer had been. They said that they had been fine. They did not need to use any of the strategies in the emergency plan, but they had brought it with them to the cottage and put it on the wall. Just having it there to look at gave them a sense of safety and security.

Communication in groups
Bente Arntzen

The problem-solving method requires adequate communication skills. Some families with a psychotic family member communicate well while others show some disturbed patterns of communication. Often disturbed communication is a result of strong emotional tension and ineffective or unsuccessful attempts at trying to tackle a host of problems. Such a strong emotional tension often produces a flood of speech that is hard to interrupt. Findings show that persons whose expressed emotion (EE) measure high, talk more than those judged to have low expressed emotion. It has also been found that patients in both of these types of family take equal time to speak. Many patients suffering from psychosis find it hard to express themselves and lack confidence and, therefore, drop out of the conversation. In families where the family members talk a lot because of strong emotional tension and the patients hardly talk at all, the family members often lose their ability to listen to each other. This results in often repeated monologues.

In a small minority of families where one of the family members has had a psychosis, the relatives' own communication is also disturbed. This can resemble psychotic thought disturbances and reveals itself in illogical pauses in the speech or strange use of words.

The way the family members communicate their thoughts and feelings has great impact on the course of illness. In a crisis, effective communication can reduce the tension in the family and promote attempts to manage the crisis and solve the problems. By the same token, ineffective patterns of communication can prevent problem-solving attempts and can contribute to an increase in symptoms.

The most typical communication problems are difficulties expressing positive and negative feelings, problems with active listening and asking questions instead of setting goals and giving feedback.

Communicating negative feelings and criticism

Family members can have different reactions to the illness. Feelings like grief, sadness, anxiety, anger, disappointment, frustration and so on are quite common. Emotional pressure builds up in the family members which can lead to inappropriate attitudes towards to the patient. Airing such feelings can relieve this pressure. When communicating negative feelings, there is a danger of expressing them as over-generalized personal attacks to which the patient is particularly vulnerable. The group leader's task is to help everyone specify the behaviour associated with the feelings and express the feeling provoked by this behaviour. By drawing attention to a particular behaviour pattern, the tendency to express over-generalized personal attacks is reduced.

When we compare the statement 'I don't like the way you cleaned up your room' to 'You are the most untidy and lazy boy in the world!' it is obvious that it is easier to accept the first statement, even if the meanings behind the two sentences are actually similar. The first statement focuses on the behaviour, while the second statement focuses on the person. When focusing on the behaviour it is easier to make things concrete, which may be a good reason for using the problem-solving method. A further example in the set-ting above might be: 'It annoys me to see how untidy your room has been for the last couple of weeks. I have asked you to clean it up several times, but I have not been able to get through to you, and now I am really frustrated. I would like to hear your opinion on it, and then we could try to find out how to solve it.'

Criticism and expression of negative feelings often arise where we want the other person to change their behaviour. Compare these two statements: 'You are a terrible cook' and 'I didn't like this steak very much. It was too raw for me. I would like it cooked a bit longer next time.' The first statement can damage the cook's self-confidence. The second statement gives us more information about how the other person would like the steak, rather than simply offering a destructive judgement. Next time when preparing a steak, the cook is likely to ask, 'How would you like your steak: rare, medium or burnt to a crisp?'

When negative feelings and criticism are expressed in the group, it is the group leader's responsibility to help the family reformulate the message into a concrete presentation of the problem. This will enable to family to opt whether and how it chooses to resolve the problem. Many group leaders find this part difficult. It takes both practice and guidance to do this the right way.

Giving help towards being understood

It is often necessary for the group leaders to try to improve the family mem-bers' ability to listen to each other. This is partly achieved by preventing everybody speaking at the same time or interrupting others. But this can also be encouraged actively.

It may be of help to point out that something which is important to a particular family member is being said and ask them to listen carefully. After the speaker is finished, the listener can be asked to repeat, in his own words, what was said. This is a good test to see how well or badly the family members communicate with each other.

The group leader should value every person's contribution, regardless of the way it is formulated. Everyone is encouraged when they feel that they have contributed. If someone is talking incomprehensibly, the group leader can say that they did not quite get the message and ask for a new formulation. If necessary, the group leader can help the person to express, in a better way, what they want to say.

Establishing basic rules

A good way of improving communication is to establish a set of basic rules and help the family members respect these.

Only one person speaks at a time

This may seem obvious, but experience shows that family members often speak across one another and try to lead parallel conversations with both group leaders. The group leader can introduce this rule by saying it is impossible for them to listen to two persons at once. It might also be observed that if there is a person in the group experiencing hallucinations, it will be hard for them to concentrate even on one conversation where only one person speaks at a time.

Several meetings may be held before the families are able to obey this rule and the group leaders have to remind the participants every time they break it. This should be done firmly but without criticizing the family members by saying, for instance 'I'm sorry, but I can only hear one person at a time. So, who goes first?'

To manage and maintain this rule means that the family members have inproved their capacity to control both their talk and the emotional pressure they experience. It also helps them show more respect for each other.

Talk to the person, not about them

It is quite common for family members to talk about a person by referring to him/her as 'he' or 'she', as if the person were not present. It is generally the patient who is mentioned in third person, particularly if he or she is non-communicative.

It is surprisingly easy, even for the group leader, to fall into this depersonalizing pattern of communication. It is important to point this out every time it happens, because it makes the person feel as if they were not actually present. This is particularly hard for patients with schizophrenia, who often have low self-esteem. Referring to them in the third person can also cause problems for patients with auditory hallucinations.

The group leader can say something like 'We will establish a rule according to which everyone who wants to say something about another person present in this room will talk directly to the person in question.' The family members will often need to be reminded of this rule. The group leader can intervene by saying something like 'What you said just now was very important, could you please say it directly to your wife?'

Another advantage with direct communication is that it tones down negative expressions. It is much harder to say 'You are very lazy' than 'He is very lazy.'

Equal time to speak

It is quite common for one family member to take up most of the speaking time, so that there is not much time left for the others, especially if that includes the patient. The group leader must explain that it is important to listen to all the family members, which means controlling the most talkative and encouraging those who are less talkative. To stop a family member in the middle of a sentence can be perceived as very impolite. The group leader must develop a style in which he is firm but tactful. They could, for instance, say 'I know you have something important to say, Mr Knight, but I also want your wife to get a chance to say something, so we will return to you afterwards.' To achieve this with humour can be very effective. Sometimes it is impossible to hold family members in check this way. A more formal structure may be necessary, for example by giving each family member 5 minutes' talking time.

Many patients are unused to contributing in conversations and often feel excluded. This could be dealt with by allowing no interruptions when the patient is speaking. The patient may feel this as an uncomfortable pressure to contribute. If this is the case, the group leader can say that it is not necessary to say anything today, but everyone will be quiet and listen in case the patient wants to say something.

Summary

- Communication can be improved by establishing a set of basic rules.
- Only one person talks at a time.
- Group members talk directly to one another.
- Everyone should have an opportunity to have equal air time.

In addition, the group members often need to be encouraged to listen actively to each other. Sometimes the ability to communicate positive feelings in respect of positive behaviour or to clarify a problem through empathic listening may be an effective strategy for solving interpersonal conflicts.

Chapter 3

Experiences

Psychoeducational family work in single-family vs multifamily groups
Anne Fjell

In this section, I will focus on some differences between the single-family group (SFG) and the multifamily group (MFG) formats and briefly dwell on some of the advantages of each of the models.

The specialists engaged in family work within the TIPS project came across some patients and families who expressed reluctance or inability to participate in MFGs. We also found that some patients and families had needs that could not be met within the multifamily group setting.

I will also briefly describe some clinical experiences and some of the reasons for providing single-family work as a preferable clinical option for some of the patients in this project cohort. The question whether family work should be conducted in single-family or in multifamily group format is much debated. Quite often this turns out to centre on the lack of alternative training and flexibility in the clinical system. A flexibility in clinical diversity will be possible only when clinicians are trained to cater fully for patients and their families.

Single-family work vs multifamily group work

When we compare the two family work models, clinical experience shows that the group model has certain clinical advantages for group members over single-family work. C.C. Bells writes:

> Against our cultural ideals of individual autonomy, agency, account-ability, and mastery, the therapists and families have to organize a counterculture that promotes beliefs in 'comprehensive treatment, protection for the subject and social acceptance of innate, biologically determined differences without stigmatization.' In this lies a reason why multifamily therapy is more effective than single–family therapy. 'One therapist and

one family are not enough to make a culture – at least one that effectively extends beyond the session.'

(McFarlane 2002: p. 359)

The idea of organizing psychoeducational family work in groups originated from the clinical observation that families meeting in hospital often show interest in one another. The idea was that multifamily groups (MFG) would answer some basic needs of such families. The opportunity of working with the issues flowing from the illness in a group with other patients and families in similar situations can provide families with a secure framework for enabling change in their situations. This may account for the fact that MFG leaders report an unusually high level of participation among group members. However, the single-family format does offer the opportunity to devote more time to individual problems within the family and to provide outreach clinical services to the family members in their natural environment so as to keep them involved in the treatment process.

Patients and their family members will often not be comfortable with attending group meetings at times when symptoms have flared up. At the early stage of the treatment, when there as yet are not established regular contacts between the patient and the clinician, as often for patients with dual disorders, the patients and their families will need support from outreach and other engagement strategies. This will be an important reason for working within the single-family model.

Reasons for not participating in an MFG

Patient's reluctance

Some patients find it very difficult to have their problems divulged to their families and becoming involved in the rehabilitation programme. We often notice that when patients and their families have faced problems like these, communication among family members may have been deteriorating for a long time.

We also know from experience that poor communication among family members often occurs when patients have not been offered help in solving problems or challenges in an acute phase of the illness. The patient's family will without help and support in this phase adjust to the situation by means of a communication style characterized by the missing information on how the patient's problems are related to the illness. In order to help the families that have been 'trapped' in a situation like this, clinicians should be able to offer an alternative outreach service. It will often take some time for the family to come to terms with the situation. Once the family members have been successfully helped to accept the need for help and support, they are invited to join a group. Meeting other families in a comparable situation provides them with further opportunities to solve daily problems in their family and feelings of guilt and shame are often considerably lessened when they listen to other families speaking about their comparable experiences.

The numbers of group members will create a less intense climate than that of the single-family group, enabling difficult problems to be dealt with. The help and support that families with similar experiences provide during problem solving will also prove a liberating experience for both patient and family members.

Prior to participating in MFGs all families have individual meetings. They need a person who can listen to their experiences of feeling helpless and overburdened. At this preparatory session, family members need to be told as soon as possible that schizophrenia is an organic illness and not caused by the family.

It is also important that family members are supplied with simple information about their important role in relapse prevention and in promoting a better prognosis.

Family reservations

Some family members may find it hard to accept the diagnostic account of their relative's psychosis as conveyed by the clinical staff. These families should be offered the single-family option to allow them to work through these challenges of understanding. It is important to clarify the family's own beliefs and help them integrate this more informed understanding of the patient's problems.

When a patient's parents reach the age of 70 or so, they are often reluctant to participate in a group. This should be respected and they should be offered outreach support to help them understand and cope with their situation.

Geographic reasons/no family

One of the most common obstacles to participating in an MFG is presented by geography. When the patient and the family members live too far apart, the family may not be able to attend group meetings every other week. When patients have no adult relatives but are themselves caregivers or single parents to young children they should have treatment offers tailored to this situation. When the patient's children are younger than 18, they should not be invited to join the MFG. Children should be offered the opportunity to talk to a clinician about their experiences of having a parent with a psychiatric illness and how this is affecting their lives.

Language reasons

Another reason for avoiding the MFG format is when the language spoken in the group is not understood or practised within the family. The family members will then be unable to make themselves clear to the rest of the MFG members and take part in the group process. Language problems may prove be an additional stress for the patients in the groups struggling with concentration difficulties. In a single-family group language challenges can be dealt with within a clinical frame tailored to meet the needs of the patient and the family members.

Some patients have a hard time dealing with the stress experienced by sitting in the same room with other people and will sometimes act these problems out in the group setting. Where these problems are revealed during the introductory meetings before group start, the patient and their family are discouraged from joining a group, but are offered support in the single-family setting.

The group climate can be easily disrupted by affective behavior and a hostile atmosphere may develop where problem-solving will be obstructed by these behavior problems. In order sort out problems like this in a MFG, the patient and the family should be invited to pause from the multifamily group and solve their problems within the more controllable setting of a single family group.

Evaluation

The single-family format for patients with psychosis will take care of problems within the family setting on an individualized level serving the explicit needs of patient and families. When patients with psychosis and their families participate in a multifamily group setting, they tend to evaluate psychoeducational multifamily groups very positively and describe this family work as 'the human touch'. It addresses, within the family setting, both individual vulnerability to psychosis and the means of avoiding situations that can lead up to a psychotic relapse. Both patients and family members express a high satisfaction at being enabled to deal with their daily experienced problems and the improvement of life quality this brings along within a family setting. For the clinicians engaged in psychoeducational family work too, this approach is experienced as a rewarding and inspiring way of working with complex clinical challenges.

Conducting educational multifamily work with younger patients
Bente Arntzen

Applying the principle of early intervention, multifamily groups have also been set up for patients below the age of 15 years. There are some obvious problems in relation to diagnosis for this age group. The patient is still in the process of development, is not fully grown, and personality may still be emerging; care is therefore needed when conducting diagnostic work. The level of motivation in these very young patients has also been shown to be a crucial factor.

When young patients come in contact with group leaders, it is usually after first onset of the psychosis. They are often through the acute stage and are not keen to start attending multifamily group meetings. Some of them claim that they are not ill and will never have relapses and hence do not see the point of participating in family work. They want to expunge the illness completely from their minds as soon as possible in order to get back to their normal life. It is therefore very necessary to stress the importance of participating in the group and that while they have put the illness behind them, the risk of becoming ill again can be much greater if they do not participate.

It is essential that the young person should be fully informed about what goes on in the group. Since they can be very distractible and have difficulties concentrating, it has proved very useful to set up role plays, demonstrating what happens at group meetings.

Getting young patients to meet each other before the group starts is also a very good form of preparation and giving them some extra time has turned out to be very useful at this motivation stage. Creativity ways should be used to find out about their lives and then provide some activities around areas of common interest. As our experience shows, inviting young patients to a meeting in an office is not the best way of helping them get to know each other. Instead, one might, for instance, go for a walk with them, go to a café, visit an art exhibition, have a pizza or soft drink and chat in a warm and relaxing atmosphere. Sometimes young patients already know each other from the young persons' ward or from the outpatient clinic.

Trying to map both warning signs of relapse and prodromal symptoms is not an easy task for young patients. For many of them it is like lifting a veil from something they want to erase completely from memory. Young patients' views about participation in the group depend to a great extent on their parents' opinion. Therefore, it is necessary to allow sufficient time to explain to parents the purpose of attending the group. This serves both to motivate the parents themselves and thereby indirectly to encourage the young people to participate.

Young patients often view participation in the group over 2 years as an impossibly long period of time. In this situation, we stress that this invitation is open to them over 2 years during which time the group leaders are available to meet participants. As for the young patients, they are free to participate for as long as they find it to be helpful. Our experience shows that most of them end up staying with the group for the whole period.

In many groups for adult patients, some will experience difficulties in taking part. This has proved less difficult in groups that involve younger patients.

Levels of participation here have been very high in respect of both relatives and patients. This may in part be because this is the age group when parents still have some control over youngsters, but we also think it is because young people enjoy participating in groups.

At first we thought it would be intimidating for them to participate in a group with 15–20 other participants and that one-to-one contact with an individual therapist would make them feel safer. But quite the opposite has proved to be the case.

Many of the young patients participating in multifamily groups could not follow regular treatment and dropped out early from individual treatment programmes, but still came regularly to the group meetings. When this was explored, many of the young people expressed the view that it was easier to be in a group rather than alone with a therapist. This is because in the group there is not so much focus on a particular patient, but attention is 'spread' across all the participants, which, they say, makes it much easier to talk about their problems. In a group it feels quite normal to have problems. At the meetings with an individual therapist the problems seem more bound up with the illness.

We think the method is also popular because at this age people are rather group oriented and can identify with other people's problems and coping strategies. Because of their similar ages, the teenagers in a group are often struggling with the same type of problems in their daily life and this contributes to a sense of recognition and identification.

Another advantage for young patients participating in the group is that they get considerable support. If one of the parents at a meeting happens to touch on a problem provoking irritation or criticism towards their son or daughter, then that individual may very often get support from the other families. After a while, the group reaches the point where they can talk about things that are difficult to touch on at home. Many families state that group discussions about problematic subjects often proceed in a calmer way than at home; conflict thus becomes less intense and less risky.

Another common situation experienced by young patients is a conflict between their need for care arising from the illness and their normal wish to be independent. For them the process of becoming independent is, in many cases, more difficult than for the healthy youth. As a result of the young patients' psychiatric illnesses their parents are often very anxious about their health problems. Patients themselves may be afraid of challenges that people normally encounter when going through the process of development and may have problems facing new experiences or testing out new things in their lives.

It may appear that the illness phase in young people is shorter than in adults. Our experience with adult patients has shown that, in the first year, most importance is attached to the problem of avoiding relapses and the focus on rehabilitation occurs during the following year. To young patients it may seem as if they recover faster than grown-up patients: their process of rehabilitation is much quicker and is not as long and hard. While this may be partly true – because it may be much easier to go back to school than to working life – it may also partly be because these young patients have not developed such a serious illness.

Running separate groups for young patients proves beneficial because many of the problems to be resolved have common characteristics; therefore, both patients and relatives can recognize themselves in each other's problems.

It is obvious that most young people feel comfortable in the group as group members and also show keen interest in each other. This can be easily seen from their strong responses when they try to solve their own and others' problems.

The group seems to be a positive environment for young people and it helps them to have their relatives there as well. It is a warm place where they can receive appropriate support while trying to learn how to live with a serious psychiatric illness.

Family work in early psychosis
Gerd-Ragna Bloch Thorsen

All over the world there is a growing awareness of the importance of early intervention in the treatment of psychosis, as well as other illnesses. The earlier the treatment starts the better the prognosis (Larsen 1999). This has produced a growing number of early outreach and early detection and treatment programmes. However, identifying a patient at an early stage is of little advantage unless effective treatment programmes can be offered. Research shows that treatment for people with schizophrenia and other psychoses should be comprehensive and should cover medication, family work, milieu therapy and psychosocial training (Borchgrevink *et al.* 1999).

Engaging the family

To offer long-term family work at an early phase of treatment can prove quite a challenge. If the patient is at an acute phase, relatives may be in shock and prone to grief and bewilderment. Very few such families have had prior experience of psychosis. It is not unusual for their knowledge of mental illness to be very limited and prejudiced or full of obsolete and irrelevant ideas. Very often it takes time for relatives come to terms with the diagnosis. And, if this is the first episode, relatives naturally hope it will be the last.

When the patient has recovered and is on medication, many relatives take too optimistic a view and think they will manage as before with minor modifications. And, indeed, some will. Contrariwise, between 20–50% of patients relapse within the first year of onset, even where they are provided with the best treatment possible (Pitschel-Waltz *et al.* 2001). It may prove difficult to educate patients and relatives about this pattern and family work tends to have a low priority in many treatment programmes (Pilling *et al.* 2002). There is also the challenge of sustaining the family's optimism while keeping in mind a realistic prognosis for the course of the illness. The task here is to help the family maintain a positive spirit, while accepting the true nature of the illness. It is therefore recommended that the family should be given sufficient time and space, but not be left alone for too long.

Sometimes the block to effective participation may lie in the patients themselves. During the first episode of the illness, patients may well have no experience or knowledge of the illness and do not want to be engaged in a long-term treatment programme; nor do they want their families to be involved. Very often, at the point of first contact with the patient, the illness has not taken serious hold. At this stage, the loss of function and of personal networks is not so widespread as to affect them significantly. This, of course, is beneficial for the patient, but it is vital for them to understand that maintaining this state will be demanding. So the task of engaging the family at this critical stage requires empathic skills. It is important to make clear to the relatives that they can leave the programme at any point, but it is prudent to invite them to give the group work a chance before they make a final decision.

Introductory talks

It is important to use time at the introductory sessions to deal with crises, early warning signs and the drawing up of the genogram. The relatives are in crisis and the need to talk and to express their guilt, fear and sorrow can be immense.

At this early stage, relatives are also very open to mapping early warning signs. Knowing such indicators can be of great help when seeking to prevent relapses. Relatives at this stage often ask themselves again and again: 'What should we have seen?', 'What could we have done?', 'We did notice that, so why did we ignore it?' and many other similar questions. Trying to systematize this and trying to gather information for later use can give some meaning to this chaotic situation. Now, they feel they can do something about it. It is not too late to improve the situation. Mapping the genogram also gives the family some valuable information. They notice connections and links; they can become aware of the impact of stressful events and can identify new resources in the family.

The educational seminar

The educational seminar with first episode patients should be conducted in a slightly different way. The relatives and the patients are kept separate. Patients in the acute phase cannot absorb all the information and spending a whole day together with four other families may prove, in most cases, too stressful. It is much more difficult to establish an accurate diagnosis when the patient is a first-episode patient. Sometimes the differential diagnosis is 'drug-induced psychosis'. We know that a lot of young psychotic patients have tried or have regularly used narcotic drugs, sometimes by way of self-medication *after* the onset of psychosis, while in some cases drugs are the primary inducing factor. And often we cannot decide which until some time has passed. At an early phase of psychosis, especially with young people, it is difficult to tell the difference between affective psychosis and schizophrenia and one always has to consider the possibility of posttraumatic, dissociative illness.

These considerations should be taken seriously when informing participants about the nature of the first episode. It is important to keep an open mind and be willing to revisit the diagnosis without losing a sense of direction. There is also the need to retain a sense of optimism.

We know that the prognosis for the first episode is better if patients receive early treatment (Larsen 1999) and we know that one-third of patients experience only a single episode. We cannot, of course, predict into which group a particular patient might fall.

Group meetings

Patients experiencing a first episode are often young and their problems resemble those common to their age group – such as difficulties with school, with jobs or in managing their leisure time. Many still live at home with their families and there may be problems in setting boundaries to their behaviour.

The challenge here is to differentiate between patterns of behaviour that are typical of the young – being self-centred, testing limits – and what can be described as clear effects of the illness.

Many families have siblings of similar age living in the family home alongside the designated patient. It can be problematic for the family to draw clear lines about unwanted behaviour for one of the children while accepting a very different standard for the patient.

Siblings often join the group meetings, especially in the early stages. However, in the course of time, many of them discontinue attendance, often because of changes in their own patterns of life. It seems to be the case that this will happen either where things are going well *or* where progress is poor. Some siblings are afraid the illness can 'strike them' as well and they try to keep their distance.

They may also feel guilty for having friends or for continuing with their schooling; while others feel that they have to be a success to compensate for the patient's situation and to provide some comfort for their parents.

When we come to the problem-solving phase of the groups, there are specific challenges in dealing with first-episode patients. In the early stage of the psychosis, the relatives and the patients often disagree in their views about the illness. The patients will often see themselves not as ill, but rather as experiencing some transient problems. They may refuse to take their medication;

and believe that because they are not ill they do not really need tablets. Refusing to attend school is also not seen as a problem; they view it more as a pause in attendance. It is therefore often a challenge for the group leaders to formulate a problem to solve that covers the problem area while not upsetting the patient. This requires the art of compromise. However, even where patients cannot admit that they are ill, they may still recognize that they are experiencing problems that need help.

While, therefore, we often encounter patients in the early stages who are passive and difficult to engage in the problem-solving approach, over the weeks of group work they become more and more engaged and also supportive of one another.

Differential diagnosis

As we have already indicated, it can be difficult making an accurate diagnosis in the early stage of a psychotic illness. In some groups of first episode patients we therefore address the problem specifically. It is particularly difficult where the patient uses illegal drugs or narcotics. Some of the drugs can mimic psychiatric symptoms and some drugs can make the symptoms of schizophrenia mimic affective disorders, as can happen with amphetamine, for example. Other drugs make affective illnesses look more like schizophrenia (e.g. cannabis). In addition we have the problem of withdrawal symptoms with drug-induced psychosis.

It is not the group leaders' task to clarify the diagnosis or to re-diagnose, but they should be in frequent dialogue with the psychiatrist or psychologist in charge of the particular case. Sometimes a patient is given a different diagnosis during the treatment period. If the patient and his family have been members of the group for some time, it is usual for the family to continue in the same group. If the patient has just started in the group, the family may change groups to one with other patients with the same diagnosis. We have even come across a case of a family being simultaneously in two groups – joining the new one with the correct diagnosis and remaining in the old one where they have started to make friends, experience support and feel at home.

Special considerations

Even though patients with first-episode psychosis share many similarities, there can also be significant differences. For patients at the early stage of psychosis, the onset can be abrupt, dramatic and frightening or it may sneak up slowly and with vague symptoms. The patient can be mildly or severely affected and the time needed to assert control over the psychotic problems may vary widely. The recovery may proceed smoothly or the patient may have many relapses during the treatment period.

Sometimes the patient is too ill to join the group meetings for much of the period. We nevertheless encourage the family to join the meetings. On a few occasions the family has been offered the chance of joining a new group after finishing the first one, when the patient has recovered and wants to participate in the family group work.

Some patients recover quickly and feel well during most of the treatment period. They may have been attending school regularly, entered and passed exams or be enjoying positive friendships. The group leaders should be flexible in these cases and invite such patients to the groups, but show understanding if other matters seem to have priority. The group, in the final resort, is not an end in itself but merely a means of helping patients take more control of their lives.

Ending the group

Sometimes patients will be in very different stages of the illness when the groups are scheduled to end, but in most cases it feels natural to conclude the groups after 18–24 months. Sometimes that marks the end of the group; but, in other cases, it may be decided to continue for a while on an infrequent basis (or the group members may even continue to meet on their own for a while). Patients will have treatment programmes elsewhere and the relatives are encouraged to work with patient and family organizations to fight for better conditions for patients and relatives and against stigma.

Psychoeducational family work applied to different diagnoses
Anne Lise Øxnevad

Most research and experience in the field of psychoeducational family work concern families where the ill member suffers from schizophrenia or related psychoses. However, there is no obvious reason why the method, with suitable modifications and adjustments, cannot be employed when working with families where the sick member has some other diagnosis. The outcomes of such work are described in Callahan and Bauer (1999).

We ourselves have tried to apply the method in work with families where a member is suffering from an affective disorder, drug abuse or anorexia.

Affective disorders

Young persons with affective disorders experience as much distress as those with other forms of psychosis. In the last few years there has been a worldwide growth in the number of early outreach and intervention programmes for people with schizophrenia. Frequently, people with affective disorders have been offered little else but medication and intervention. What we know now is that the onset of affective disorders occurs much earlier than was formerly believed and that the prognosis is often no better than in other forms of psychosis. Research has shown that psychoeducational work for patients with affective disorder and their families can produce good results and that this kind of treatment should therefore be offered to this group of patients as well (Goldstein and Miklowitz 1994).

We decided to offer multifamily group work for this class of patient and the programme was adjusted to suit their special needs. Since more patients with affective disorder than with schizophrenia are able to marry and start families, should we mix married couples with parents and grown-up children in the same group? Should we mix people with both manic and depressive episodes with those suffering from major depression only?

We decided to keep married couples in one group and we assigned parents with manic-depressive children to another. We also decided that patients should have had at least one manic episode to be included in our programme. The introductory sessions are held in the same way as described earlier but, of course, there are often more family members with affective disorders to enter on the genogram: it can also be hard, especially for parents, to recognize that the child may have inherited the illness from 'my side of the family'. If some other family members, an uncle, a grandfather or one of the parents themselves, happen to have had the illness, the family is often better informed about the illness than the relatives of patients with schizophrenia. Sometimes this knowledge can give hope since the ill relative may have coped rather well with the condition; sometimes, however, this direct experience can be frightening. It is also important for the group leader to offer realistic hope and explain the favourable outcomes psychoeducational family work can produce. The educational seminar, of course, has to be 'tailor made' to fit this diagnostic group. The topics discussed are those that relate to the diagnosis and treatment of affective disorders, but in general covers the same areas. The early stages of groups involving couples can be highly significant but challenging. Those with affective disorder often have good pre-morbid functioning. Spouses of the patients may experience feelings of guilt in different ways, as does the patient: 'I brought the illness to this family. I hope the children will not be affected' is a thought that can often be expressed. The couples will provide clear indications that the illness affects the whole family. It is, therefore, vital that each spouse receives the same information.

The group leaders are likely to sense higher levels of emotion and liveliness in these groups. Family relationship issues are raised more often, as well as the problem of stigma and shame. What shall I tell work colleagues? What to tell the neighbours? What information shall we give to the children and at what age? These questions are more often heard in affective groups rather than in groups including patients with schizophrenia. Many participants confirm that this kind of treatment has worked better for them than anything else offered earlier. As a family they are able to feel, think and reflect about the illness along similar lines. Attending the group has saved many marriages and has been very important for children since the parents have been able to apply their knowledge and problem-solving strategies to the home environment. The results in the groups for parents have been just as positive as in the groups for grown-up children. Parents become aware of their responsibilities towards the sick person and recognize the contribution they can make. This does make a real difference when it comes to prognosis and relapse. They regard the group as a place where they can openly express their ideas and concerns.

Sometimes it feels helpful if the patients attending the group are at different stages of their illness. Seeing someone in a more positive phase can give hope. Participants also remark that the group helps the family to pinpoint early warning signs so that the patient can take the measures necessary to prevent relapse; this tends to give the whole family a better understanding of the illness.

Drug abuse

Very many young patients with schizophrenia use or abuse drugs. This can function as a means of self-medication or simply offer an escape from the illness. In the groups we still use the problem-solving method to address this issue. This has encouraged us to use the method for treating young persons who present with substance abuse as their main problem. Exposure to the multifamily programme can help the whole family reduce negative emotions and cope more successfully with the situation. Of course, it would be better if the patient stopped using drugs altogether, but modifying the patient's behaviour and improving relationships between family members can be of great help. When working in a group, the relatives experience mutuality and understanding from the other families. The families get help to set limits on unacceptable behaviour and can learn from one another. The patients are more likely to listen to other group members than to their own families and, by reducing stress in the families, the need for drugs is similarly reduced.

Anorexia

We have also applied the method in our work with people suffering from severe anorexia, although on a very limited scale. Of course, the educational seminar needs to be modified to suit the diagnosis, but additional challenges have also been experienced. The method has been designed for people with schizophrenia and is very suitable for people with cognitive deficit and concentration problems. This is not the case for people with anorexia. The family atmosphere can sometimes become very tense. The parents may show a high degree of over-involvement which is understandable when they have experienced their child almost starving to death.

Mapping early warning signs is not as easy. The patient may sometimes wish to share these with the group leaders, but keep them secret from the family. These early warning signs are the patient's way of coping, as well as a sign of their illness and they do not want to give this away, at least not at an early phase of the illness. We also see second-generation eating disorder patients, who have grown up in a family preoccupied with diet and healthy living. Families with severe eating disorders tend not to talk about their feelings and emotions and, according to one theory, the symptoms replace these missing words and emotions. This can also be a challenge in the groups (Dare and Eisler 1997). However, our experience with this group is very limited and it is too early for us to draw any firm conclusions.

Chapter 4

Drug abuse and psychosis

Working with families of people suffering from psychosis and substance misuse
Christine Barrowclough

Introduction

In the last 25 years many controlled trials of family interventions for people with schizophrenia have been published. The efficacy of such work is now well established and it has been consistently demonstrated that there are considerable patient gains from such interventions, not least in terms of reducing relapse outcomes (Mari and Streiner 1997; Pilling *et al.* 2002; Pitschel-Waltz *et al.* 2001).

However, despite the fact that a significant and increasing number of schizophrenia patients are known to misuse drugs and alcohol, there are few reports of family interventions that address the particular issues arising in families where a member has a substance problem in addition to the psychosis. This chapter attempts to review the limited literature available about family issues with dual-diagnosis clients, before describing a family treatment approach focusing on drug and alcohol problems in psychosis clients.

Many people who care for a person with severe mental illness report considerable personal stress and burden as a consequence (Barrowclough *et al.* 1996). Copello (2003) discusses the stresses experienced by families of individuals who have primary substance misuse problems and suggests that the presence of the dual problems of psychosis and substance use creates the potential to expose families to a wider range of stresses than either problem alone. Studies have shown that the rate of substance use in schizophrenia is high, with estimates for community samples of recent or current abuse in the range of 20–60% (Lehman and Dixon 1995), suggesting that large numbers of families are experiencing very significant levels of complex problems.

However, there has been little investigation into those carers who have the additional strain of dealing not only with schizophrenia but also with substance misuse. There are a few available reports from studies in the USA, all of which indicate that family stress has a high prevalence in dual-diagnosis households. For example, two small sample studies (Alterman *et al.* 1980; Sciacca and Hatfield 1995) of psychosis and substance misuse reported that family problems were evident in approximately 50% of cases. In the latter study, the most salient problems were patient denial of the problem and patient decline in health. These concerns are likely to lead to both frustration and anger with the patient's attitude and behaviour and also anxiety about their well-being. Such conflicting emotions are suggested in the descriptive account of dual-diagnosis carers reported by Mueser and Gingerich (1994).

A case note study of 121 persons admitted to hospital with a schizophrenia diagnosis (Kashner *et al.* 1991) gives further evidence of family stress in this context. Those with a substance abuse problem were nearly four times as likely to have family members with 'severely disturbed affect'. This finding is consistent with the report that dually diagnosed clients expressed lower levels of satisfaction with their families than clients with just a psychiatric disorder alone (Dixon *et al.* 1995). The latter study looked at 179 patients with a DSM IIIR axis 1 current primary mental disorder of whom 101 had a current additional psychoactive substance use disorder and concluded: 'Inner-city mentally ill patients with a co-morbid substance use disorder perceive lower levels of family satisfaction than comparable patients with severe mental illness only' and 'Of note patients with a co-morbid use disorder did not report less frequent family contacts, which made their family potentially no less available' (Dixon *et al.* 1995: 457).

In addition to the supporting evidence in the literature, many clinicians working in mental health services will have witnessed the difficulties and dilemmas facing relatives of people with a dual diagnosis. It is well documented that drugs and alcohol use are correlated with many worse outcomes in schizophrenia (Maslin 2003) including illness complications such as suicide, poorer compliance with treatment, more inpatient stays, violence and poorer overall prognosis (e.g. REFS). Services are often at a loss as to how best to treat these patients who are seen as presenting many challenges since the evidence base for effective management is very limited (Ley and Jeffrey 2004). How then are relatives expected to deal with the problems? How can conflicts be avoided in homes where patients are intoxicated or using street drugs, spending family income on these substances and apparently compromising their chances of restoring their mental health? In these circumstances, the family stress generated is likely to affect not only the well-being of the carers, but it may also have an impact on the course of the illness itself and on outcomes for the client. Many studies have found that high expressed emotion (EE) in carers – a measure of affect and behaviour directed at the patient – is associated with an increased risk of relapse (Butzlaff and Hooley 1998). Although little is known of the reasons why some carers develop high EE attitudes, a consistent finding in the literature is that high EE relatives tend to assume that the client can control their problematic behaviour and symptoms

(Barrowclough and Hooley 2003). On these grounds, Turner (1998) suggests that high EE will be prevalent in families where there is a substance-abusing individual, especially since dominant societal attitudes in western culture tend to blame substance abusers for their behaviour. If this prediction is correct, then we would expect to see raised levels of high EE in dual-diagnosis households and, hence, such patients would have additional relapse risks.

The Manchester Dual Diagnosis Intervention study

The Manchester Dual Diagnosis study (Barrowclough *et al.* 2000a; Haddock *et al.* 2003) was a randomized controlled trial designed to evaluate the effectiveness of a treatment programme with schizophrenia patients who had either drug or alcohol use problems. The aim of this trial was to investigate whether the programme of interventions had a beneficial effect on illness and substance use outcomes over and above that achieved by routine care. The focus of this chapter is on the family intervention component of the pro-gramme. However, having been presented with details of the study design and the full treatment programme, the reader will, it is hoped, be able to place the family work in context.

Inclusion criteria for the study were as follows:

1   a non-affective psychotic disorder: schizophrenia or schizoaffective disorder according to ICD-10 and DSM IV criteria
2   meeting DSM IV diagnostic criteria for substance dependence or misuse
3   in current contact with mental health services
4   age 18–65 years
5   a minimum of 10 hours' face-to-face contact with the carer per week
6   no evidence of organic brain disease, significant concurrent medical illness or learning disability.

A final sample of 36 patient–carer dyads took part in the study. The patients were mainly male (92%) and young (mean age 31.1 years). Multiple substances were commonly used; 19 patients had both drug and alcohol misuse and poly-drug use was frequently found. The drug used by most patients was cannabis (22 patients), followed by amphetamines (10), cocaine (four) and heroin (four). The demographic characteristics of the sample would seem to be in accord with gender and age biases found in larger stud-ies: substance use in schizophrenia (as in the general population) is more likely to be found in young males (e.g. Mueser *et al.* 1990). Similarly, the substance use profile of the study sample matches the type of substance use most prominent with schizophrenia patients. A recent review of prevalence studies for substance use in schizophrenia (Blanchard *et al.* 2000) reports cannabis to be the most frequently used drug; alcohol use frequently occurs with drug use; and multiple substance use is common. Alcohol is the most frequently found substance of abuse in this population (Smith and Hucker 1994).

The planned intervention period was 9 months, with sessions taking place in the carers' and patients' homes, except where clients expressed a preference for a clinic-based appointment (one individual CBT intervention, no carer interventions). All patients in the study (treatment and control groups) were allocated a family support worker from the voluntary carers' organization Making Space. The services of this support worker included: information, benefits advice, advocacy, emotional support and practical help. The frequency and nature of support worker contact was decided by mutual agreement between carer and support worker. For clients in the treatment group, the intervention attempted to integrate three treatment approaches: motivational interviewing (MI); individual cognitive behaviour therapy (CBT); and family or carer intervention (FI). The rationale for this treatment synthesis was based on a number of a priori assumptions detailed elsewhere (Barrowclough *et al.* 2000b). Briefly, first, there was the expectation that the majority of patients would be unmotivated to change their substance use at the outset, hence interventions to enhance motivation would be necessary; second, that symptomatology might be implicated in the maintenance of substance use while in turn the drug and alcohol use might exacerbate symptoms and thus psychological interventions to address symptoms would be important; and, third, that family factors may have a bearing both on symptomatology and continuation of drug or alcohol use, hence the need for family interventions. Thus we assumed an underlying model for the maintenance of the problem whereby motivation to use substances and symptomatology and environmental stress in the social milieu were locked in an iterative and mutually reinforcing process.

Overview of the intervention

The intervention began with the motivational interviewing phase which consisted of five weekly sessions designed to assess then enhance the patient's motivation to change. With the introduction of the individual cognitive behaviour therapy (CBT) at week six (or earlier if appropriate) the motivational interviewing style was integrated into subsequent CBT sessions. Where clients remained unmotivated or ambivalent about substance use, motivational work was continued. 'Booster' motivational work was appropriate if problems with client commitment became apparent at a later stage in the intervention. Once client commitment was obtained, changes in substance use were negotiated on an individual basis and might involve reduction, stabilization or abstention. The individual CBT took place over approximately 18 weekly sessions, followed by six fortnightly sessions. This phase included a detailed assessment of psychotic symptoms and techniques to reduce the severity and distress of persistent positive symptoms, techniques to enhance self-esteem, to improve depressed mood, as well as interventions to improve knowledge and understanding of the illness and the medication. Relapse prevention strategies were used both for psychotic symptoms and to maintain changes in substance use.

Following assessment of both patient and carers, shared goals were generated which become the focus of conjoint patient/family sessions. Details of the motivational and individual CBT components have been given elsewhere (Barrowclough *et al.* 2000b; Haddock *et al.* 2003). The remainder of this chapter will focus on describing the family intervention in more detail.

Characteristics of carers in the study

To give a context to the family intervention, some descriptive statistics about the carers in the study may be helpful: 27 were female and 9 male; and the mean age was 51 years (SD 12.12). In terms of relationships, the majority (24, 67%) were parents, six (17%) were partners and the remainder consisted of sibling (one), grandparent (one), landlady (two) and ex-partner (two). Of the 32 households where consent was given for Camberwell Family Interviews which were assessed for expressed emotion (EE) (Leff and Vaughn 1985), 66% (21/32) were rated high EE. In terms of subjective burden or distress, 53% (19/36) fulfilled criteria for 'caseness' on the 28-item General Health Questionnaire (GHQ) (Goldberg and Williams 1988). In summary, the profile of these families fulfilled the predictions of the available literature on this area reviewed earlier: by and large they were a highly stressed group of people who were predominantly high EE status.

Family intervention

The family intervention consisted of between 10–16 sessions, some of which took the form of integrated family/patient sessions, some of which might involve family members alone. The family intervention was strongly influenced by the motivational component of the programme. In working with people's motivation to change their substance use we adopted the stages of change model developed by Prochaska and DiClemente (1986). The model describes how in the process of change people pass through states or stages of readiness ranging from pre-contemplation (the person does not perceive themselves as having a problem or needing to make a change), contemplation (both considering change and rejecting it), preparation/action (being motivated to make change) and maintenance (taking steps to keep up the change). Motivation is conceptualized as an internal state of readiness which can be influenced by external factors. One way of influencing change readiness is through the therapist's style of interviewing and 'motivational interviewing' (Miller and Rollnick 1991) was used in this study to facilitate increased motivation for change. The importance of this intervention component was borne out by the characteristics of the sample. Using the University of Rhode Island Change Assessment Scale (McConnaughy *et al.* 1983), 78% (28/36) of the sample were found to have low motivation at pre-treatment assessment, defined as being *pre-contemplative* or *contemplative*. Key concepts employed in this style of interviewing are: ambivalence is normal; resolving ambivalence is the key to change; responsibility for problems and their consequences is left with the client; and change efforts are not started before clients have committed themselves to particular goals and strategies.

A key underlying assumption of the family intervention was that the patient's motivational state as regards changing their substance use could be influenced by the family environment. The intervention sought to promote a family response that was consistent with the motivational interviewing style and the stages of change model. Hence aspects of such a response would be: responsibility for problems and their consequences needs to be left with the client; confrontation about substance use may create more resistance to change; and family help will be most effective when it matches the stage of change of the client. It should be emphasized that the stress reduction approach of the generic family intervention model (Barrowclough and Tarrier 1992) and motivational enhancement approaches were in complete concordance. The approaches shared a common framework about the kind of help from family members that was likely to be most effective. Take, for example, patients who are at best only at the *contemplative* stage of change. The family intervention in such cases might be directed at helping relatives to appreciate that attempts to try to make someone change their substance use, on one hand, or, on the other, to buffer the consequences of the use, would be counterproductive. If responsibility for change is to be left with the patient, the family may need to embrace the deliberate strategy of not persuading, cajoling, or even encouraging clients to stop drinking or using drugs. This approach was promoted in the educational and subsequent interventions as an active and positive strategy of detachment, rather than a passive and negative way of behaving. It emphasized that the family need to leave it up to the client to make changes. However, at the same time, it is good to communicate personal feelings about substance use; and to set boundaries and limits on the extent to which family members will tolerate the substance abuse having adverse consequences on the family life. Such limits would include not rescuing clients from the consequences of drug/alcohol use: for example, not bailing them out financially if they blow their money on drugs/alcohol; not covering up for their periods of drunkenness; establishing reasonable house rules about acceptability of behaviour with age-appropriate sanctions that the relative is willing to carry through if rules are broken. For patients who have accepted the need to cut down or abstain from using substances and who have started to make change, the emphasis on client responsibility would also endorse the relative supporting changes once they have happened, but not the relative attempting to initiate change.

The general approach to cognitive behavioural family intervention used in the study has been documented (Barrowclough and Tarrier 1992). It begins with a detailed assessment of family problems and needs elicited from structured interviews, supplemented where appropriate by questionnaires. Following from this assessment a collaborative problems and needs list is formulated which would typically include:

1 issues concerning the relatives' understanding of the illness
2 relatives' distress
3 coping difficulties
4 dissatisfactions with particular aspects of the patient's behaviour
5 restrictions and hardships that the relative is suffering as a consequence of the illness.

Additionally, family strengths would be highlighted. Using the problem list as a guide, the interventions to address the family needs are then structured around three components:

1 education
2 stress management and coping strategies
3 goal setting to promote patient and relative change.

In the dual-diagnosis study, using the motivational framework, problems associated with substance use were identified in the assessment phase, highlighted in the problem formulation and addressed in each of the intervention components. An outline of these adaptations of the family intervention is now given.

EDUCATION

Brief family educational interventions alone have no effects on patient behaviour and do not appear to affect long-term changes in family well-being or relatives' management strategies (see Barrowclough and Tarrier 1992: chapter 5, for a brief review). It is argued that they are best construed as setting the scene for bringing about family change (Smith and Birchwood 1987). In cognitive behaviour therapy terms, they attempt to begin to 'socialize' the family into the stress/vulnerability model of psychotic illness. A simple model of psychosis is presented whereby enduring biological vulnerability may be exacerbated by environmental stress. The aim is to communicate to families, on the one hand, a sense of realism about the long-term risks of continued problems and illness exacerbations and, on the other hand, a sense of optimism. Such optimism is derived from an understanding that by working together it may be possible to improve the course of the illness and improve patient functioning by taking illness (vulnerability) and environmental (stress) factors into account. Information that is incorporated into this framework includes: details of the patient's illness symptoms (positive and negative); the causes of psychosis; treatment and the role of medication; the course and prognosis; and the role of the social environment including how their own behaviour may influence outcomes. The content of sessions is modified to accommodate relatives' current understanding and models of illness. There is also flexibility about which family members attend, although invariably patients would be encouraged to attend some of the sessions to enable them to contribute to describing the experience of psychosis. An interactive and collaborative style is used, acknowledging the relatives' viewpoint while sensitively working to offer alternative explanations where appropriate.

In assessing relatives' understanding of substance use in schizophrenia, the Knowledge About Schizophrenia Interview (KASI) (see Barrowclough and Tarrier 1992) was modified for dual-diagnosis families by the addition of sections asking about relatives' understanding of drug and alcohol issues. As with other sections of the KASI, the questions attempt to assess how helpful or unhelpful the beliefs they hold are likely to be, in this context in terms of supporting a motivational approach. 'Helpful' information and beliefs which might be targeted at the information sessions include those likely to lead to a less blaming attitude. These are ones which associate the substance use more with the illness (less with factors personal to the patient themselves); and which acknowledge that it is difficult for the patient to change without help from others and exceptional effort on the patient's part. Hence ideas incorporated into the educational sessions on substance use include:

- Substance use in schizophrenia is very common.
- Drugs and/or alcohol in themselves cannot cause psychosis in the absence of additional vulnerability factors.
- Drugs and alcohol use can sometimes worsen symptoms and have a negative effect on the illness, but this needs to be balanced alongside the patient's perspective of the positive effects. Such positive or at least 'benign' reasons why patients abuse substances include: helps to social-ize, helps to cope with symptoms, gives pleasure, patient does not have many pleasure opportunities and ameliorates the negative effects of medication.
- Substance use is not completely under the patient's control – change can be made but this requires exceptional and long-term effort on the part of the patient.
- An understanding of the stages of change model and how a person's current position in the change cycle will determine the kind of support that is most helpful. When people are currently not ready for change, persuasion serves only to set their minds against change.
- Change is not an all-or-nothing process and it is usual for people to go

through a cycle of cessation and relapse and back to thinking about change, then preparing for change, several times before achieving permanent abstinence.
• The best strategies for helping patients are non-confrontational, non-critical, non-intrusive.

The need for emphasizing some of these issues is illustrated in the following case example:

Steven was a young man aged 21 years who had recently been discharged from his second hospital admission. During the psychosis he had developed complex delusional beliefs of a strongly religious and threatening nature, became very withdrawn and prior to the second hospital admission had attempted suicide. He began smoking cannabis at university and continued after his first admission and his subsequent return to the family home. His parents thought that the delusional ideas were 'drug induced' and attributed his lack of activity, withdrawal and just about all his problems to cannabis. There were frequent arguments at home – his father felt he had 'brought the illness on himself' and could not understand why he 'chose to make himself worse'.

The early educational sessions attempted to help the parents understand the role of cannabis in the context of Steven's life and his psychosis and to generate some less blaming attributions about his substance misuse. Why had he developed the psychosis? From Steven's accounts, his cannabis use at university did seem to be closely associated with and to precede the onset of his symptoms. However, his use had been no greater than the rest of the majority of his peer group. Steven was the only one to develop a psychosis which suggested that there was something about him – a sensitivity – which made him vulnerable to its effects. This fitted in with what we know about the 'stress/vulnerability model' of psychosis. Cannabis was one stressor or trigger. Other stressors which might trigger a psychosis are life events such as life changes or losses, such as relationship breakups or bereavements. The impact of cannabis on him would have been difficult for anyone, including Steven himself, to predict. Why did he continue to use? His parents were encouraged to think of the reasons why many people continued to take or do things that were not good for them in the face of 'good' advice, e.g. to smoke cigarettes, overeat, stay in bad relationships, drink too much alcohol etc. and the idea of the stages of change and the normalcy of ambivalence were introduced. With Steven's permission, information was fed back to his parents about his thoughts and beliefs – how intensely distressing and powerful his voices continued to be, how he felt stigmatized by the illness and the fact he could not return to university. Steven's reasons for substance use might be better understood in this context – it helped him relax, take time out from his thoughts and fears and to feel 'normal' and like his peers. Why do people with mental illnesses misuse substances more than the rest of the population? The costs which were clear to his parents – 'making the illness worse' – were not apparent to Steven or to other people in his situation because they could not imagine being well again and their self-efficacy for change was reduced by their experiences of the psychosis.

While attempting to cultivate a less blaming view of the substance misuse, the education sessions also emphasize helpful strategies. The general message is that the best strategies for helping patients are non-confrontational, non-critical, non-intrusive and do not require self-sacrifice on the relative's part and focus on positives rather than negatives. In place of arguments, basic house rules about acceptability, with sanctions that can be followed through if rules are broken (e.g. about taking drugs at home) are suggested as an alternative:

- Similarly, not rescuing the patient from the consequences of drug/alcohol use (e.g. not covering up for their drunkenness, not doing things the patient neglects to do because of their drugs/alcohol use).
- Making time for oneself is prioritized, while sacrificing one's own well-being to the problem is unlikely to help anyone in the long term.

One or two educational sessions were dedicated to communicating these ideas to the relatives. The precise content would be determined by the KASI assessment and other information about the relatives' viewpoints. The style of information giving would be as interactive as possible.

As noted earlier, these points of information were viewed as setting the scene for exploring possible ways the family might change their responses to substance misuse. Given that many of the ideas were new and did not fit with their personal models of construing the substance use, the information alone was not expected to change beliefs or behaviours. Care had to be taken not to give families the impression that there was implicit criticism of their current perspective or behaviour. The commitment and experience of the carers and their enormous contribution to supporting the well-being of the patients was frequently acknowledged. Engagement then collaboration were key strategies for the intervention. Common problems associated with the substance use identified time and again in the education sessions were:

1   Relatives tending to blame patients for making their problems worse through substance misuse.
2   Underestimating the patient's symptomatology in relation to schizo-phrenia and tending to attribute all the problems to the substances.
3   Relatives being reluctant to stand back and leave responsibility for

change with clients, feeling that this would be tantamount to condoning substance use.

STRESS MANAGEMENT

While the education sessions offered information, ideas and general advice, the stress management component of the intervention aimed to introduce change and to thereby reduce intra-familial stress in the household. It focused directly on the situations associated with stress, attempted to conduct a cognitive behavioural assessment of these situations and, from this assessment, to collaboratively explore ways of reducing stress. The transactional model of stress was used to conceptualize problems in the household, whereby stress was seen as a transaction between the patient's symptoms and behaviours and relatives' attempts to cope with these problems. Without denying the very real problems relatives often have to deal with – disturbed behaviours, behavioural deficits, and in this context problems associated with drugs and alcohol use – the model underlined the importance of relatives' reactions in determining stress responses: how the relatives construe situations and what they do about them may not only fail to resolve the problem, but in some cases serve to maintain or exacerbate it. Examples here in the context of dual diagnosis would be relatives' attempts to deal with a patient's excessive drinking through verbal persuasion not to drink or through arguments when the patient returns to the house intoxicated. Such attempts to reduce the drinking, although well intended, may fail to have an impact on the drinking or may in fact indirectly increase the patient's motivation to drink where alcohol is used to cope with the patient's stress or where arguments against drinking increase the patient's resistance to change as suggested by the motivational model. Moreover, given that the relatives' energies are invested in non-productive attempts to change the patient's behaviour, they are likely to get more frustrated, dissatisfied with the patient and stressed themselves in the long term.

In collaborating with family members on how best to deal with stressful situations it is helpful to consider stress reduction techniques as having two forms. If we take the view that the difficulties are a transaction between the problem itself and how the relative appraises or responds to it, it follows that there are two possible avenues to reducing the stress response. First, ameliorating the problem itself through interventions that would decrease or eradicate the problem behaviour. These might focus mainly on working with the patient through psychological approaches to manage the symptoms or, in the case of dual diagnosis, through motivational work on substance use. Second, to help the relative to manage negative emotions, thoughts and behaviours associated with or triggered by the patient's problems. Interventions might include reappraising the patient's behaviour, helping the relative to increase the time spent on their own interests and to use anxiety reduction techniques such as relaxation or challenging negative thoughts. In practice, most interventions involve both problem-based coping and emotion-focused coping and take into account the particular family situation.

The following case example illustrates some of the issues outlined:

The patient, Susan, is a woman in her late 20s with a 6-year history of psychosis. There have been frequent hospital admissions and she has persistent paranoid ideas. Susan's fears make it difficult for her to go out. She has a group of local friends who drink quite heavily and smoke cannabis. She lives with her mother who at assessment believed her daughter's illness was caused and maintained by drug use. Her mother goes to great lengths to try and find occupation and distraction for her daughter with the aim of keeping her safe at home and away from contact with her friends. As a consequence the mother's life is very restricted. She has given up her job and has become isolated, not wanting to leave her daughter alone in the house. Despite these sacrifices, the daughter does meet her friends and uses cannabis several times a week, spending all her benefits on drugs. This is the source of arguments between mother and daughter and the mother suffers considerable financial hardship since Susan pays nothing towards her keep.

One of the issues targeted in the education sessions was the need for Susan to take sole responsibility for the drug use. In a gentle, non-confrontational manner the stages of change model was used to help the mother see that Susan was only at the beginning of the contemplative (or 'thinking') stage. Susan was just beginning to think about some of the negative aspects of cannabis use (the costs, fears of long-term health problems), but still in Susan's eyes the good things about smoking cannabis outweighed the bad. In other words, Susan was not yet ready for change. By the same token, the mother's actions assumed Susan was ready. Hence her mother was getting very frustrated when her attempts to help Susan not to use drugs met with resistance and did not have any impact on the problem.

In the stress management sessions, her mother was encouraged to reappraise the help she was giving Susan in the light of the stages of change model. Through such a guided discovery process, she was helped to see that there were more disadvantages than advantages in maintaining this role of attempting to control the substance use. For example, the surveillance of Susan's behaviour and the arguments did not affect the drug use. Indeed, the arguments might be increasing Susan's resistance to change. At the same time, there were personal costs for the mother in terms of deterioration in her social life, finances and mood as a consequence of her sacrifices. In joint sessions with Susan it was agreed that the mother should experiment in leaving Susan alone some days and monitoring the consequences. This required some gentle challenging of the mother's catastrophic beliefs about what might happen if her daughter were left to her own devices, alongside some help in problem solving how to distract herself from her own anxious thoughts. At the same time, the mother was encouraged to set some clear limits about Susan's behaviours associated with the drug use. Susan agreed not to smoke cannabis in the house and her mother made it clear that she would not provide Susan with cigarettes or cash once she had run out of her benefits money. She also began to ask Susan for a contribution towards her keep.

The first stress management session in this intervention was attended by the mother alone. Once the mother's permission was obtained to try out these new strategies, Susan attended and was encouraged to contribute to the planning. As in most similar situations, Susan was fully aware of her mother's stress and hardship and welcomed the opportunity to attempt to resolve some of the conflict and support her mother. However, the negative impact of increased financial constraints arising from her mother's demands for more money from her helped to increase Susan's ambivalence about her cannabis use. It was important that this was highlighted in subsequent individual sessions with Susan which attempted to enhance her motivation to reduce substance use.

One of the difficulties encountered in the study was resistance of family members to reducing the amount of control they perceived themselves to have over the substance use. The way this control was exerted was through methods such as managing the patient's money, searching the house for drugs and disposing of any found, expressing dissatisfaction with their drug use or attempting to keep the patient occupied in the hope that they would not feel the need to seek out substances. Although by their own admission the substance use remained problematic, family members had real concerns over what might happen if they released this control. Getting the family to see new ways of coping as 'experiments' did facilitate change, which could be reinforced when they found that releasing 'control' did not have obvious adverse effects. Moreover, the patients themselves often encouraged these changes, expressed a desire to help the relatives have more time for themselves and offered reassurance that the controls were unlikely to influence their own substance using behaviour.

A CONSTRUCTIONAL APPROACH TO PROBLEMS: GOAL SETTING

The chief aim of the goal setting component in the family intervention is to improve the social functioning of the family members (Barrowclough and Tarrier, 1992). Using the format of goal planning and seeing the whole family together, the aim is to teach the family a constructional approach to the problems of family members. This entails seeing problems as needs which might best be met through promoting positive behaviour change. An indirect aim is to reduce family stress by directing their attempts to assist the patient towards methods which are constructional and have a high chance of success, hopefully replacing previous unsuccessful attempts which focused on trying to eradicate problem behaviours. In the context of the dual-diagnosis families, this emphasis was very important and helped to counter the feeling that to be asked to leave responsibility for substance use with the patient was to be required to do nothing. It was presented as an opportunity to channel all the carers' efforts to help into plans that might promote positive client behaviours (rather than into fruitless arguments and frustrated attempts to control the substances).

This component was closely linked to individual CBT patient sessions and was a forum for addressing problem areas identified as common to both patients and relatives during the initial problem identification and formulation stage. Additionally, it offered the opportunity for families to assist with patient plans and goals developed in the individual sessions.

The chief assessment tool is a strengths/problems/needs list which identifies, on the one hand, a person's abilities, interests and resources and, on the other hand, difficulties issues or problems. Combining the individual and the family work, common problem areas were highlighted and both family members and the patient were encouraged to contribute further items. Example of strengths/needs list for a man (Paul) using amphetamines living with his mother (Linda) and younger brother (Keith) is shown in Table 4.1.

In the strengths/needs list in Table 4.1, the asterisked items formed part of the original joint problem list, while the other items were elicited through later assessments and discussions. As may be seen from the example, the assessment tries to identify issues that may benefit from co/joint working. The problems are translated into needs which are responses to the question, 'If the problem were resolved, what would the person be doing?' Working on the needs of all family members prevents undue 'pathologizing' of the patient's problems and encourages joint working.

Once the list is constructed, the needs are reviewed and rank ordered by the family in terms of priority and feasibility in the short term. It is important that all the patient needs are of relevance to the patient or the exercise may be construed as critical and one sided and unlikely to achieve change. Relevance may be achieved by restructuring a problem which is a priority to the relative so it has increased patient relevance. For example, Linda is very dissatisfied with Paul's inactivity, while for Paul it is the boredom that he finds unacceptable and hence the two may be linked to a common goal. Similarly, while it is Linda who feels that Paul pays insufficient towards his keep while frittering money away on drink and amphetamines, Paul is upset by the arguments; and while for Linda the issue is about feeling overburdened with housework when Paul seems to have nothing to do, the issue for Paul is autonomy. Needs are by no means independent and clear links between needs may be used to

Table 4.1 Example of a strengths/needs list

Strengths	Problems/issues/areas for change	Needs
Paul's interests/abilities: music, driving, TV, books, seeing friends, playing football, cycling; cooking skills, computer skills, enjoys helping others	Linda has a restricted social life	Linda needs to increase social activities away from family
Linda's interests/ abilities: job (nursing); reading; walking; dressmaking; cooking; seeing family	*Linda tends to do all the domestic chores and Paul would like to be more independent	Linda and Paul need to plan to share some domestic tasks
	Paul has difficulty going out alone	Paul needs to increase his confidence in getting out
Resources: close, caring family; other relatives want to help; Linda has local friends	*Paul spends a lot of time inactive and is bored	Paul needs to increase his interests and activities
	*Paul and Linda argue about money Linda and Paul feel Keith misses out on time with the family	Paul and Linda need to resolve money issues Paul and Linda need to find ways of spending more time with Keith

advantage: for example, Paul's inactivity might be addressed by his doing things outside the house or even doing things outside the house while spending more time with his brother.

After identifying the need, the strengths list is scanned for approaches that might be used to meet the need; a goal is specified in clear behavioural terms (and possibly broken down into easily attainable steps); patient and relatives' participation in the goal step is reviewed – whether this constitutes an active (i.e. facilitating) or passive role, the latter being desirable if the relative's response is intrusive or fosters dependency. At further sessions the goal is reviewed.

A potential problem in the goal-planning sessions was that the family members might easily fall back into the old arguments about drinking and drug use. Hence it was helpful to raise that potential difficulty at the beginning of sessions and to encourage agreement that drug and alcohol issues per se would not be discussed (although associated problems such as finances might well be on the agenda).

Outcomes and conclusions from the study

The full results of the study are reported elsewhere (Barrowclough *et al.* 2000a; Haddock *et al.* 2003), but there is now good evidence for the efficacy of the combined programme into which the family intervention was integrated. The study demonstrated that an intensive treatment programme incorporating a family intervention resulted in significant improvement in the main outcome of patients' general functioning (General Assessment of Functioning (GAF) scores) when compared with 'treatment as usual' and that this improvement was maintained at 18 months' follow-up. There were also significant benefits to patients in terms of some secondary outcomes including negative symptoms; although other improvements in positive symptoms, in symptom exacerbations and an increase in days abstinent from drugs and alcohol, which were evident at 12 months' follow-up, were not maintained at 18 months. For carers, there were trends for a reduction in identified needs and in both subjective and objective burden. The lack of statistical significance may have been due to the small sample size, although equally we need to acknowledge that the intervention was relatively short and longer term, more intensive interventions may be required for some families where the interactions between substance use and psychosis led to entrenched problems and extremely high levels of family stress.

Little information is available to indicate what percentage of schizophrenia patients with substance use have contact with families or whether family contact patients have a different profile of substance use to those without. It is possible that those patients who have maintained close family contact may have less severe problems than those who have not maintained contact. A comparison of the characteristics of our group with a matched sample of patients who did not have significant carer contact showed that the groups did not differ on a range of variables including symptom and illness severity and type of substance use, although they were significantly older than our study sample (Schofield *et al.* 2001). It is possible that this indicates that carer relationships of those patients who have psychosis and substance use problems may deteriorate over time and carer contact may be reduced.

Our clinical observations suggested that the levels of substance use may be lower in patients living with or in close contact to relatives. This may arise when relatives control substance use consumption in the ways we have described. Although this control may have short-term benefits in terms of fewer substances consumed, the situation may inadvertently contribute to decreasing the patient's readiness to change simply from the fact that the negative consequences of substance consumption are limited or buffered by the well-meaning attempts of the family to protect the patient from the harmful effects of increased use. Certainly, feelings of frustration over failed attempts to persuade the patient to change were very prevalent among family members. Carer assessments indicated that there were high levels of stress in the households. This suggested that not only was carer well-being compromised by the 'double burden' of schizophrenia and substance use, but that an adverse social environment was a contributory factor to symptom exacerbations in the patients.

The study reported here has demonstrated that it is possible to improve the illness course and reduce substance use in dual-diagnosis clients through a multi-component psychological and psychosocial intervention. Although the indications are that such multifaceted treatments may be required to effectively impact on the complex and challenging problems of this client group, in the longer term, research is needed to examine the relative efficacy of different components of integrated interventions. Further studies are also required to examine the long-term outcomes for both family members and patients.

Acknowledgement

This work was supported by West Pennine, Manchester and Stockport Health Authorities and Tameside & Glossop NHS Trust R&D support funds; and Making Space, the organization for supporting carers and sufferers of mental illness. The author acknowledges the contributions of the research team and the therapists involved in the trial described here, including Gillian Haddock, Nicholas Tarrier, Shôn Lewis, Jan Moring, Rob O'Brien, Nichola Schofield, John McGovern and Ian Lowens.

Chapter 5

Implementation of psychoeducational family work

Qualifications group leaders need
Gerd-Ragna Bloch Thorsen

When setting up and conducting psychoeducational multifamily groups, there are certain criteria that need to be met. First, we need skilled professionals who *want* to conduct this work. At least 3 years of healthcare education and 2 years of practice within the field of psychiatric care are recommended. Practice should include experience in working with psychosis and psychotic patients. We also need the approval of the administration or decision makers and a consistent methodology both for educating group leaders and for evaluating outcomes.

Attitude

Working as a group leader in multifamily groups is rather different from other psychiatric treatment methods. It is very different from a psycho-analytic or psychodynamic approach and it is also different from the traditional belief that the professionals are the experts and the patient must accept the treatment offered unquestioningly.

If a therapist has been trained in psychoanalytical methods, then the use of interpretations, the focus on transference and countertransference and the reliance on the patient's presentation of material have to be set aside. These skills can, of course, still be applied in other settings, but they should not be combined with the psychoeducational methods. From the very outset stress is placed on equality, partnership and the pursuit of a common goal. The group leaders are, of course, responsible for administering and running the group, but in doing so they tend to disclose more about themselves than is usual in other psychological treatment methods. Disclosure about oneself, one's family and hobbies, serves not only to signal that we are on equal terms with participants, but also to minimize transference reactions. In psychoeducational work, the goal is not to try to find causes and scape-goats or explore traumas and feelings; instead, the work is concentrated around problem solving. There is no focus, in traditional psychiatric practice, on identifying and working through feelings. Group leaders must have this pragmatic attitude even if they can observe connections and hidden conflicts. For a psychodynamically trained therapist this can sometimes prove difficult and takes both additional training and supervision.

Knowledge

In addition to the appropriate attitudes, workers need accurate knowledge about the illness and its treatment. It is important for group leaders to be able to educate the families in these subjects as part of the educational seminar. In the group, many questions will be raised about the illness, the treatment programme, the medication and its side effects. Even though it may not be helpful to answer all the questions that arise, appropriate knowledge in the field is still required.

Structure

For this treatment approach to prove effective, the methodology must be strictly followed. The families should be taken methodically through the different elements of the programme in an empathic and caring atmosphere. Sometimes a family member may talk too much or become aggressive. The group leader should be able to deal with such problems as well as knowing what to do where families are too passive or withdrawn. The agreed structure should be unfailingly observed, especially as it provides a support structure for those suffering from psychosis or cognitive deficits. It also serves to control anxiety and insecurity.

Record keeping

Records of the group meetings need to be maintained, for example: Who attended? What kind of problems emerged? Whose problems did the group address? Was there any specific incident or problem that dominated the group meeting?

After each meeting the group leaders should stay behind, discuss the meeting and complete the appropriate records.

How to learn the method

A range of training programmes is available for professionals working in the sphere of psychoeducational treatment methods. While it is possible to attend one programme and apply it to another context, the best method is to concentrate on one model and learn that thoroughly. In Norway, it has been decided to focus on a common national educational programme. This ensures that there is no doubt about the qualification of group leaders or the prestige and significance of the psychoeducational method.

To be accepted for the programme a participant must have at least 3 years' training in healthcare, plus 2 years' psychiatric practice, including working experience with psychotic patients. The programme consists of 60 hours of education, which can be provided as a 2-week, full-time course or as a single-day programme at intervals over a longer period of time.

The training programme covers an understanding of psychosis, diagnostics, crisis theory and education about family stress, as well as basic theory on group leadership. Research in the field of psychosis, expressed emotion (EE) and dual diagnosis are explored. The whole range of treatment programmes is covered, including psychotherapy, milieu therapy, medical treatment and so on. Participants in the training engage in role plays, and are required to lead parts of the educational seminar. It is important that they should have teaching skills, since the psychoeducational method is based on a pedagogic approach. In addition, during the delivery of the programme, they are required to teach the educational seminar and possibly on other occasions also.

The training programme includes at least 1000 pages of literature on the issues in that particular field.

Before leading a group on their own, the trainee leaders should visit other groups at least twice. It is recommended that inexperienced group leaders should start their first group supported by a more experienced leader.

Supervision

Candidates must run a group for 2 years under supervision before they are entitled to recognition as multifamily leaders. Group meetings are held every fortnight and there is monthly supervision. Although this may be on an individual basis, group supervision is usually preferred. Normal practice is to use the problem-solving method during supervision in order to get it 'under one's skin'.

During supervision, the group records can be examined to see the kinds of problem that were encountered; this will reveal how the candidate approached the problem resolution. It is very important for candidates to be helped to assimilate and integrate the problem-solving method. Regular and repeated practice of the method is required.

In our region, it is necessary to undergo supervision for 2 years while running a family group in order to attain the status of group leader. The supervision should be conducted by a recognized multifamily therapy supervisor. The aim of this is to enhance knowledge about the psychoeducational method.

Educational skills, problem-solving skills and group leadership skills should also be developed. Candidates should also be able to reflect critically on their own practice and this again will contribute to higher quality in the actual multifamily work as well as facilitating quality assurance processes.

The treatment elements in family work are *problem solving*, enhancing *communication skills* and *communication* and the focus of supervision should, therefore, be placed on these elements.

Group leaders are responsible for bringing their own material to supervision.

Experience shows that by using the problem-solving method in supervision the candidate gains confidence in using and following the method. Role play and video material are also used.

We have chosen to conduct supervision in groups. This is in part a more efficient use of resources but also allows expertise to be pooled. Doctors, nurses, social workers and psychologists sharing their experience together can also be a very useful way of learning from one another.

Part of the supervision process addresses organizational matters (Where? When? How? Who?). Research elements can also form part of such a process, and it is important to allow enough time to deal with such issues.

A form of register is also necessary. Questions such as what to register and how much detail to go into depend on whether this is regular clinical work or research work. Nevertheless, a minimum of records should be kept; the scheme shown in Figure 5.1 gives an example.

Choosing a co-leader

When running a group for 2 years it is vital that the two group leaders get on well together. When involved in running a group every fortnight, usually in the afternoons, it is important to have a good colleague who is trusted and respected. It is an advantage if the two have slightly different professional backgrounds and can cover a wide range of experience and knowledge, as well as problem areas. A psychiatric nurse and a social worker often make a good match.

How to implement psychoeducational family work in an established system
Anne Lise Øxnevad

Many studies have been carried out which show the positive results of including a patient's family in the treatment process. While the family is often an important resource to the patient, relatives have frequently been left in isolation from any contact with the health services. Between 1992 and 1996 the researcher Tor Ketil Larsen carried out a study on the duration of untreated psychosis (Larsen 1999). He wanted to find out how long it took before people with psychotic symptoms received any kind of relevant treatment. In this connection, he also asked about service providers' contacts with relatives.

NAME	Present	Subjects addressed	Other questions

Family 1

NAME	Present	Subjects addressed	Other questions

Family 2

NAME	Present	Subjects addressed	Other questions

Family 3

NAME	Present	Subjects addressed	Other questions

Family 4

Figure 5.1 Sample protocol showing minimum of records to be kept.

There was a clear consensus that relatives had good contacts with the psychiatric healthcare system (Rogaland Psychiatric Hospital); this, however, turned out not to be the case: only a few of them had received any form of organized help.

Through the 'Early Intervention in Psychosis' (TIPS) project, a standard-ized treatment protocol consisting of three main elements – psychotherapy, medication and family work – has been tested.

The TIPS project was started in 1997. Prior to this, there had been a long preparation phase dealing with the family work element. A thorough review was conducted of the many research studies dealing with family work with patients suffering from serious mental illnesses, particularly schizophrenia. In the final analysis, William McFarlane's psychoeducational model based on multifamily groups was selected. His results showed the lowest relapse rate after one year. The model was also the least resource demanding, because it involved gathering four to six groups together with two group leaders. The patient also participates in the group meetings. A pilot project provided the opportunity to test the model, because, among other things, appropriate resources were available.

Psychoeducational family work is a treatment approach that has been used in many countries, both in Europe and in the rest of the world. Besides William McFarlane, others such as Ian Falloon, Julian Leff, Gerard Hogarty, Douglas Reiss and Carol Andersson are among the eminent practitioners who have developed psychoeducational family work as part of the treatment of serious mental illness.

Although the Rogaland Psychiatric Hospital chose the model developed by William McFarlane in respect of patients suffering from psychotic illness, it seems probable that psychoeducational family work can be extended to patients with other diagnoses (see pages 84–87 in Chapter 3).

One of the goals of the TIPS project is to assure the quality of treatment and to implement family work as part of the total programme offered to young people with first-episode psychosis. The professional management of the hospital also endorsed this model as a permanent treatment effort after the project ended. The hospital management need to be aware that the approach involves some important elements:

1   The hospital management should become familiar with the methodology and its research evidence, leading to a quality assurance approach to the treatment of patients with first-episode psychosis. This should be grad-ually expanded to other groups of patients.
2   The hospital should consider it their responsibility to cooperate with patients' families/relatives and to provide the resources required such as financial support and suitably qualified personnel.
3   The hospital should contribute to the establishment of a positive profes-sional climate, providing guidance to the group leaders and offering the necessary professional development.

The choice of the multifamily group model with patients participating is time-consuming work. Yet it is less demanding than running single-family groups. Most time is spent on the introductory conversations. Before starting a multifamily group we need to allocate approximately 70 hours of professional contact time, divided between relatives and patients – including the time needed for the education seminar. This is followed by meetings held approximately 3 hours every second week for 2 years, not counting possible crisis interventions and meetings with the patient's therapist.

Just as we emphasize the importance of starting the treatment of psychotic patients at an early stage, our experience also underlines the importance of the family work. In some cases, for a variety of reasons, several weeks or even months had elapsed before the group leader met the family. At this point, some of the families had been in a crisis for a very long time indeed and many had had little or no contact with the health services. Although their experiences varied, many felt rejected, alone and helpless. They had many questions but had received few answers.

One family said the following when they met the group leader for the first time: 'In the hour we've spent with you we have received more information than we have in the two months our daughter has been hospitalised.' This tells us something about the family's needs: their thirst for information and their anxieties.

By offering the family both factual information and cooperation, we can avoid deadlocked, negative conflicts. This, in turn, will benefit the patient. The goal should be for the group leader to contact the family within a week.

The introductory conversations with the family require some flexibility on the part of the group leaders. To offer the family meetings in the afternoons can influence how quickly the multifamily group can get started. This might lead to additional expenditure for the hospital in respect of overtime pay and time in lieu; so it is important to clarify all these points prior to the start of the programme.

However, receiving overtime pay and time in lieu has proved an important motivation for group leaders, since the work is demanding and it requires motivation to return to work late in the afternoon or evening.

To run psychoeducational family work involves cooperating with the patient and family. The group leaders also rely on cooperation from the patient's individual therapist so that there is a common pursuit of the treatment goals. Through family work, it is possible to free the patient's individual therapist from some of their routine functions, so that they can concentrate primarily on the patient. For such work with psychoeducational family groups, it is a basic assumption that the group leader should have experience in working with serious mental illnesses and have relevant knowledge in related areas.

The ability to cooperate with the patient's family requires the maintenance of non-blaming attitudes on the part of the leaders.

In connection with the TIPS project, the Rogaland Psychiatric Hospital launched the 'Family School'. This is an educational course within the psychoeducational family work programme, involving 60 hours of theory (including role play). This was necessary both to recruit group leaders and to assure the quality of the work. Part of the quality assurance inherent in this method lies also in the continuous guidance provided to the group leaders.

To maintain the motivation of the group leaders, it was necessary to encourage a sense of commitment and ownership through seminars, workshops and meetings. This facilitated the development of a living peer group, which could provide mutual inspiration to colleagues in their work.

How the family can help and support
Anne Lise Øxnevad

Much of the material in this section is informed by the book *Schizophrenia and the Family* by Carol M. Anderson, Gerard E. Hogarty and Douglas J. Reiss published in 1986. This book is an important contribution to psychoeducational work the world over.

Even though this section especially addresses patients with schizophrenia and their relatives, families with a relative with some other diagnosis will also find these guidelines useful. Many of our young patients have additional drug problems and setting limits on unwanted behaviour is an important topic for these families as well. What we know from experience is that most families with a member who abuses drugs struggle with setting limits; however, this applies not only to drug abuse, but to acceptable behaviour, use of money, participation in family activities and so on as well.

Usually, the more knowledge patients have about the illness they are suffering from, the more they are willing to cooperate with medical staff. If the relative suspects or has some inkling that something is wrong, then it is important to help the individual find out as much as possible about the illness. There will always be those who will not accept that something is wrong with them. Unfortunately, this may be part of a psychotic disorder. To admit to being ill is not made any easier by all the myths around mental illness that still exist in our society. In addition, it may be hard to accept an illness where the evidence of diagnostic tests cannot be presented as is the case with physical illnesses, for instance X-ray diagnostics, blood tests etc. The family acquires knowledge about the illness by taking part in the treatment programme and becomes better equipped to understand and help the ill person:

- *Year One*:
  In the first year after a psychotic breakdown or hospitalization, the aim is to avoid relapse and gradually resume normal functioning according to one's role in the family.
- *Year Two*:
  The aim of the second year is to start a gradual process of resuming

education or work, in addition to resuming and developing one's social functioning *outside* the family.

What expectations should the family have?

Many families believe that work is the best medicine. When the patient is recovering or has just been discharged from hospital, the family are concerned with getting the patient active and encouraging him. But recovery is a laborious and time-consuming process. The family members are easily disappointed and can become dejected if they do not bear this in mind. Recovery often comes in fits and starts, sometimes two steps forward and one back.

Some families will feel that the illness is not improving when the patient appears passive and withdrawn over a long period. To some patients this stage actually constitutes a protective factor. They need to remain on this plateau for a period of time to avoid deterioration in their condition. It should not be regarded as stagnation or as a reason for family members to despair.

Some psychotic patients do not need to be hospitalized, but may be treated as outpatients. For this group of patients, too, there may be significant variation in the pace of their recovery and in control over their symptoms. But what is common to all of them is that they may experience a period characterized by inactivity and lack of motivation.

Many patients with psychosis also have an increased need for sleep which the family may experience as burdensome. The reason for the increased need of sleep is often a combination of the illness itself and the prescribed medication.

The family need to be aware there may be a period characterized by increased need for sleep, social withdrawal and limited activity. This is a normal process and the patient should not be viewed as 'lazy'. This is often a difficult period for the family; they are often impatient and want the patient back on track again.

Most patients emerge from this phase gradually and, little by little, become more and more active and well functioning. Some patients avoid the withdrawal phase and quickly get back to their earlier level of functioning. It is therefore important that the family do not compare their ill family member to anybody else.

Avoid overstimulation

Given what we know about the patient's vulnerability and reduced stress tolerance the family can participate in the recovery process by reducing the stress at home. There are different kinds of stress, one of them being *interpersonal stress* which is found in all families.

Some families have a higher level of internally expressed emotions and conflicts than others. Such internally expressed emotions accompanied by a climate characterized by conflict can contribute to a relapse. Conflicts, criticism, intense contact and exposure to many people at the same time can be difficult to handle for the patient. Criticism and conflict between the family members in general, and the patient in particular, can prove a negative factor. Every attempt should be made to reduce criticism, nagging, rejection, quarrelling and conflicts. Even 'well' relatives may also find such family friction uncomfortable, but they can usually handle it. For the patient, however, this will be more difficult and may even slow down the recovery process.

In some families, there may be an excessive degree of involvement with the patient. This shows itself in too high an intensity of encouragement and support. Some patients experience the family as taking over all responsibilities and making decisions concerning their lives. Of course, the family members are well intentioned, but their actions deprive the patient of responsibility and sense of self-autonomy. Sometimes the family members prove incapable of dealing with the ill person and therefore become involved in a negative way.

It is important for the patient to have the opportunity to withdraw and spend time alone when the need arises. The family should be very alert to this and respond immediately when the patient signals that he or she has had enough of activities and social company. It is important that the family accept the patient's refusal to participate without criticism or pressure.

For many families it may be difficult to know how to deal with the patient. They may, for example, fail to distinguish between over- and understimulation. When the patient feels comfortable and able to take part in decision making, it is usually a good experience for the rest of the family as well.

Set limits

Some families wear themselves out; others take on too much and gradually lose their capacity to cope with the responsibilities they have undertaken. While most families have ground rules for everyday living, they need to show adaptability so that daily life may function in the best possible way.

To limit stimulation does not mean being indulgent or allowing the patient to do whatever they please at the family's expense. We all know the saying, 'Anything for a quiet life'. It may be difficult to explain that explicit rules and boundaries can contribute to domestic peace and reduce conflicts, thereby lessening the likelihood of overstimulation. We shall explain this in more detail.

Whenever the patient feels overwhelmed by inner chaos, we know that he/she will feel even worse if there is also *outer* chaos. A year after her first hospitalization one patient put it like this: 'A psychotic breakdown feels like an inner earthquake. It takes time for the inner landscape to heal.' Here we can see what the patient means by 'inner chaos' as we all know what the aftermath of an earthquake looks like.

Outer boundaries that are reasonable, clear and unambiguous are support mechanisms to the patient and can contribute to reducing inner chaos. Clear boundaries are also important to prevent other family members from being exposed to too much stress and pressure.

The following list offers a number of points to use as guidance for families trying to set reasonable and effective limits to unwanted behaviour:

1   It may be prudent to set up a *minimum of rules* at an early stage. When laying down the rules try to separate behaviour that is merely irritating from that which is intolerably annoying.

> After the onset of his illness Peter lost interest in his appearance. While he still maintained personal hygiene, he did not always consider the colour combination of his clothes. This especially upset his mother. But the entire family noticed that he was very restless and when the family gathered around the television Peter would pace around the living room. This was unbearably annoying for the entire family. The fact that Peter did not dress the way his mother wished was an irritation that his mother could live with. But when Peter paced around the living room all evening, this became an unbearable irritation to the entire family. In this situation it may be sensible to agree a rule with Peter that when restlessness takes over, he is allowed to pace around the hall or some other room.

Threats and violence should never be accepted. Other forms of behaviour should be entertained to deal with the family members' reactions.

2   Set limits *clearly and explicitly* and without protracted debate. Try to avoid detailed explanations or discussions about why certain boundaries are set. Try to say assertively: 'This behaviour is not acceptable.'

3   Make your demands *concrete*. It is often difficult for patients when the demands made of them are too generalized. An example of a general demand may be: 'You should help more about the house.' Try to say instead: 'You should make your bed every day' or 'It's your job to cook the potatoes.'

Earlier we talked about how patients often struggle with their lack of personal initiative. You may, therefore, have to remind them about their duties. By setting concrete tasks you are letting the patient knows precisely what is expected.

4   It is important to set limits at an *early stage*. If the family members try to 'hold out' at any cost, they will often become more and more frustrated and irritated. This may lead to anger and negative statements about the

patient. In the end, the patient may feel rejected by the family. This is much more stressful than having to accept demands and boundaries.

5   Try not to use *age* as a guide to setting boundaries. It may seem unreasonable to set up rules and duties for grownups in their 20s or 30s. But if the patient cannot live up to normal expectations it is important that the family should help them out. And it is no real support just to wait for them to 'grow up'.

6   Before any boundaries are set or any demands made, the family should ask themselves: 'Will we be able to maintain this?'

     Inconsistency only makes thing worse for the patient. Avoid threats. If the family have problems with boundaries and demands, conflict resolution etc., then they should seek professional help. Making reasonable demands and limits can be difficult.

7   Expect boundaries to be *tested*. It is important to be consistent over time to achieve steady and lasting results. The patient should understand that his/her needs cannot always be the centre of the entire family's attention. We place special emphasis on setting limits because it is very important to create a sense of structure and a positive emotional climate in the family. It is particularly important to set limits on psychotic, violent and bizarre behaviour because this is both intolerable for the rest of the family and unacceptable to society.

Do not deny the person's assessment of their reality, but try to communicate that this is not the way you understand it and that what is happening to them may be symptoms of an illness. Be honest to yourself and to the patient in accepting that they are suffering from an illness and that their experiences are not rooted in reality. It is important not to try to convince patients that they are wrong. It is not possible to set the same limits to inappropriate thoughts as we can to unwanted behaviour. Psychotic delusions can never be disproved by argument. It can be difficult to set limits on psychotic delusions, particularly of a paranoid nature.

For example, setting out to explain that the patient's perceived persecutors do not really exist is unlikely to be effective. Trying to help patients 'escape' from persecutors might merely persuade them that someone in the family is in league with the persecutors. In cases like this, family members should not respond to what the patient says or does, but to its *emotional content*. Try saying: 'I understand how difficult it must be for you when you feel persecuted like this, but we are here, and we will stay with you.' The offer of emotional support will help the patient to feel more secure.

The family often looks for positive change – to see the patient making progress in many areas. It is more helpful to concentrate on one or two areas and allow time for change to happen. It is particularly difficult for the family to accept what we call 'negative symptoms'. Passivity and lack of contact are such negative symptoms. Clearly, members of the family will want to have patients back to their former selves. If, however, they bear in mind that passivity, withdrawal, lack of contact and increased need for sleep usually decline with time and that it is not a demonstration of active rejection or laziness on the part of the patient, it may prove easier to avoid criticism, arguments and a sense of hopelessness.

Appropriate communication

It has become clear in our work that the way we communicate with patients who have or have had a psychosis is very important. A clear and appropriate form of communication will have a direct impact on the process of recovery. It is therefore important that the family develop such appropriate forms of communication. The main principle of effective communication with this group of patients is to keep messages clear and simple without unnecessary detail and without exploring issues 'in depth'.

Take responsibility for your own communication and accept what others are saying

In many families it is not uncommon to complete other people's sentences, to presume or to practise 'mind reading'. This may confirm patients' assumptions that others can read their thoughts. Further, it may disturb the process of communication and will be very hard for anyone who has just experienced a psychotic episode. Therefore it is important that both the family and the patient should speak for themselves and avoid interpreting or probing what others might mean. We need also to respect the statements of others, even when we are in disagreement with them.

The core psychotic symptom can be described as a gradual loss of the ability to differentiate oneself from one's environment. The patient's psychological defences break down and they become uncertain of their identity and of the nature of the environment.

As a consequence, some patients feel that others can read their thoughts and even 'steal' them. Some also feel that they are controlled by others. By talking for oneself and avoiding 'mind reading' it is possible to help patients feel more secure about who they are and acquire a sense of defined self-boundaries. When patients feel more or less chaotic, for instance when they are having difficulties 'processing impressions', they can be perceived as being 'slow witted'. It will often take time to get an answer from the patient and there may be many hesitations. This may often lead to the family answering for the patient or completing the patient's sentences. It will not help the patient, since they will not be responsible for their own communication. At the same time patients may feel that they are not regarded as grownups. Parents often forget that their children have already become adult, independent persons. The parents should therefore try to be patient and wait until the ill family member has had their say and, at the same time, respect this, even if they disagree.

When the family are in crisis, avoid touching on emotional themes, such as religion, politics, sexuality, moral behaviour etc. The family may be in turmoil and may easily confuse or overstimulate the patient. It may also be difficult for the patient if the family members try to explain or find meaning in the psychotic statements. The patient will be desperate when not understood. It is therefore important that relatives try to limit psychotic communication by encouraging and helping patients express themselves in plain and clear language.

Offer support and encouragement

The family will often worry about the patient's possible relapse. Once they have learnt to recognize the relevant warning signs, they should pay particular attention to these. This will sometimes lead them to concentrate on negative aspects in the patient's behaviour and overlook the progress the patient is making. All people need positive feedback and this is particularly important for patients who are struggling with low self-esteem. When the family members do manage to express positive sentiments, even where their underlying feelings are less optimistic, this can contribute to reinforcing the patient's self-esteem. When the family manages to recognize small positive changes by making positive comments, this will also serve to strengthen the interdependence between family and patient, which, in turn, will create a better atmosphere in the family environment.

Support for medication

It is important that the family support the medication regime. Many patients have ambivalent feelings about antipsychotic medication. They recognize that the medicine makes them better when they are ill and reduces distressing symptoms, but they are often negative when it comes to taking medication over a longer period. For many patients it is important to continue to take a maintenance dose, even after the symptoms have disappeared.

When they feel well they do not see any reason for taking the medication any longer. Some want to discontinue because of side effects and sometimes because it does not seem 'cool' to take medicines. These are among the reasons why patients tend to abandon medication.

For many patients it is important to continue with their medication in order to prevent the development of a chronic condition. The family's attitude is, therefore, of decisive importance in supporting the patient's compliance with the prescribed medication. If the family are positive and actively encouraging, this will critically influence whether or not the patient continues to take medication.

If the family is to collaborate in this respect, then it is important that they are given proper and adequate information about the effects and side effects of any particular drug and its significance for the patient's recovery. It may be helpful to quote research outcomes which demonstrate that patients who do not receive medication based treatment have a relapse rate of 80% during the first year.

Network maintenance

Maintaining social contact with people other than one's closest relatives requires health, energy and time. Where there is a sick member in the family, the effort needed to cope with the problems caused by the illness may lead to isolation and a loss of contact with the world outside. The family seem to have sufficient of a burden imposed on them by their relative's illness and they can therefore easily find themselves trapped in a vicious circle. By being aware of this at an early stage families can seek to avoid dropping out of social contacts and try to maintain a reasonable quality of life.

Patients will often have the same difficulty. In many cases, their only relationships are with their close family and they often feel entirely dependent on them for contact and support. Since the patient is so dependent on the family this may increase stress and conflict in the family. Hence part of the treatment will be to help the patient establish contacts and take part in various activities outside the home.

The timing of patients' return to work or school will depend on the overall clinical picture and the level of stability in the control of the psychosis. Some patients will not be able to take on regular work or resume their normal studies, but they *will* be able to function pretty well at work that is adapted for them. Health or occupational services should assist patients in finding suitable work to make their life as meaningful as possible.

It is important to stress that the family must learn to recognize the patient's warning signs of relapse so that they can be of help and support if these symptoms develop. The family will also be able to help the patient in line with their crisis plan.

In most cases the family is a positive resource for their sick relative. Most want to be of help and support. It can, however, be difficult to know how to be of help if you do not have enough knowledge about the illness. Through participation in psychoeducational multifamily work the family will gain knowledge and receive advice and guidance from the group leaders and other group members. Through problem solving the family will get help to manage their everyday life with the ill family member and thereby achieve substantial and lasting recovery.

Advice to relatives

- Lower the patient's expectations.
- Formulate individual goals.
- Set limits to threats and violence.
- Discuss issues explicitly and clearly.
- Plan the day.
- Gradually increase the patient's responsibilities, increasing his/her independence.
- Support medication.
- Learn to recognize the patient's relapse symptoms/warning signs.
- Solve problems by using the problem-solving method.

Words from the family
The Bratthammer Family*

Expectations

When we were asked to participate in this project we knew very little about it but understood it could be important to us. We wanted to learn more about the illness and how we could live with it in our daily life.

We thought that 2 years was too long a period of time. How many problems could one have over 2 years?

The introductory conversations gave us a good idea about the whole thing, especially warning signs; and mapping them was useful for preventing relapse. We were also curious to see if other families had the same experiences as we did.

The family TIPS day, which provided us with a lot of useful information, was a start on that road. By having information one feels stronger and ready to meet the challenges that are to come.

Group meetings

At first our son felt a bit diffident in the presence of the rest of the group.

It gave us some sense of security that we had already met group leaders.

It turned out that we had quite a lot in common with the members of the other families; even if the families were very different they proved to have the same issues and problems which we had been trying to manage in our daily life. Sometimes it felt a bit uncomfortable to witness someone from another family being discussed, but it was useful, too.

After a while we felt safer among the group and talked with more ease.

* The editor writes: We are grateful to the Bratthammer family who consented to contribute and to use their real names.

It was good to see that the problems people had did not depend on their status, family structure or resources. As relatives we felt that it was good and useful to learn about what may trigger another episode of psychosis – something that helped us question when, and if it were necessary, to 'pressurize' our young son.

Another thing is that we, as relatives, learnt to set limits on ourselves and get rid of unnecessary feelings of guilt.

When the 2 years came to an end it was a bit difficult to accept that we had finished. We could very well have continued but with longer intervals between meetings.

Four years later

During the 4 years that have passed since we ended our group meetings, our son has settled in his own flat, he has got a job and is living a nearly completely normal life. He stays in good contact with the family and friends; he had only one little relapse that was discovered at a very early phase as we already knew the warning signs. He came into treatment quickly and the period of hospitalization was very short.

Conclusion

Participating in the project has been very useful for us. We manage our daily life much better and the family does not fear another relapse so much. We feel that we are prepared to take action in situations where the warning signs show, in order that the relapse should not be as serious and be of short duration. This reassures us and gives us energy to concern ourselves about things other than the illness.

With kindest regards.

Stein-Ove Bratthammer
Heidi Bratthammer
Turid Bratthammer

Bibliography

Addington, J., Collins, A., McCleerly, A. and Addington, D. (2005) The role of family work in early psychosis, *Schizophrenia Research*, 79, 77–83.

Alterman, A.I., Erdlen, F.R., McLellan, A.T. and Mann, S.C. (1980) Problem drinking in hospitalised schizophrenic patients, *Addictive Behaviour*, 5: 273–276.

Anderson, C.M. (1983) A psychoeducational program for families of patients with schizophrenia, in W.R. McFarlane (ed.) *Family Therapy in Schizophrenia*, New York: Guilford Press.

Anderson, C.M., Reiss, D.J. and Hogarty, G.E. (1986) *Schizophrenia and the Family*, New York: Guilford Press.

Antonovsky, A. (1991) *Health, Stress, and Coping*, San Francisco: Jossey-Bass.

Antonovsky, A. (1987) *Unraveling the Mystery of Health*, San Francisco: Jossey-Bass.

Barrowclough, C. and Hooley, J. (2003) Attributions and expressed emotion: a review, *Clinical Psychology Review*, 23: 849–880.

Barrowclough, C. and Tarrier, N. (1992) *Families of Schizophrenic Patients: Cognitive Behavioural Intervention*, London: Chapman & Hall.

Barrowclough, C., Tarrier, N. and Johnston, M. (1996) Distress, expressed emotion and attributions in relatives of schizophrenic patients, *Schizophrenia Bulletin*, 22 (4): 691–702.

Barrowclough, C., Tarrier, N. and Johnston, M. (1994) Attributions, expressed emotion and patient relapse: an attributional model of relatives response to schizophrenic illness, *Behaviour Therapy*, 25: 67–88.

Barrowclough, C., Haddock, G., Tarrier, N., Lewis, S., Moring, J., O'Brien, R., Schofield, N. and McGovern, J. (2000a) Randomised controlled trial of motivational interviewing and cognitive behavioural intervention for schizophrenia patients with associated drug or alcohol misuse. Unpublished paper.

Barrowclough, C., Haddock, G., Tarrier, N., Moring, J. and Lewis, S. (2000b) Cognitive behavioural intervention for individuals with severe mental illness who have a substance misuse problem, *Psychiatric Rehabilitation Skills*, 4: 216–233.

Bateson, G. (1972) *Steps to an Ecology of Mind*, New York: Ballantine.

Beck, J.S. (1995) *Cognitive Therapy. Basics and Beyond*, New York: Guilford Press.

Beckmann, K. (1998) Attitudes of ward staff towards families of patients suffering from schizophrenia. Unpublished dissertation, Department of Psychology, University of Tromsö.

Bentsen, H. (1999) *Psykososial Behandling ved Psykoser*, in T.S. Borchgrevink,

A. Fjell and B. Rishovd Rund (eds) *Psykososial Behandling ved Psykoser*, Oslo: Tano Aschehoug.

Blanchard, J., Brown, S.A., Horan, W.A. and Sherwood, A.R. (2000) Substance use disorders in schizophrenia: review, integration and a proposed model, *Clinical Psychology Review*, 20 (2): 207–234.

Borchgrevink, T.S., Fjell, A. and Rishovd Rund, B. (eds) (1999) *Psykososial Behandling ved Psykoser*, Oslo: Tano Aschehoug.

Brewin, C.R., MacCarthy, B., Duda, K. and Vaughn, C.E. (1991) Attributions and expressed emotion in the relatives of patients with schizophrenia, *Journal of Abnormal Psychology*, 100: 546–554.

Brown, G.W., Bone, M., Dalison, B. and Wing, J.K. (1966) *Schizophrenia and Social Care: A Comparison Follow-Up Study of 339 Schizophrenic Patients*, Maudsley Monograph No. 17, London: Oxford University Press.

Budd, J. and Hughes, I.C.T. (1997) What do relatives of people with schizophrenia find helpful about family intervention?, *Schizophrenia Bulletin*, 23 (2): 341–347.

Butzlaff, R.L. and Hooley, J.M. (1998) Expressed emotion and psychiatric relapse: a meta-analysis, *Archives of General Psychiatry*, 55: 547–552.

Callahan, A.M. and Bauer, M.S. (1999) Psychosocial interventions for bipolar disorders, *Psychiatric Clinics of North America*, 22 (3).

Caplan, G. (1964) *Principles of Preventive Psychiatry*, New York: Basic Books.

Copello, A. (2003) Substance misuse and psychosis in context: the influences of families and social networks, in H.L. Graham, A. Copello, M.J. Birchwood and K.T. Mueser (eds) *Substance Misuse in Psychosis: Approaches to Treatment and Service Delivery*, Chichester: Wiley.

Dare, C. and Eisler, I. (1997) Family therapy for anorexia nervosa, in D.M. Garner and P.B. Garfinkel (eds) *Handbook of Treatment of Eating Disorders*, New York: Guilford Press.

D'Elia, G. and Orhagen, T. (1991) Psykopedagogiska familieinterventioner vid schizofreni, En oversikt, *Nord. Psykiatr. Tutskr*, 45: 53–59.

Dixon, L., McNary, S. and Lehman, A. (1995) Substance abuse and family relationships of persons with severe mental illness, *American Journal of Psychiatry*, 152: 456–458.

Falloon, I.R., Boyd, J. and McGill, C.W. (1984) *Family Care of Schizophrenia*, New York: Guilford Press.

Falloon, I.R.H. (1986) Family stress and schizophrenia: theory and practice, *Psychiatric Clinics of North America*, 9 (1): 165–181.

Falloon, I.R.H. and Schanahan, W.J. (1990) Community management of schizophrenia, *British Journal of Hospital Medicine*, 43: 62–66.

Friedman, S., Smith, L. and Fogel, D. (1999) Suicidality in panic disorder: a comparison with schizophrenic, depressed and other anxiety disorder outpatients, *Journal of Anxiety Disorders*, 13 (5): 447–461.

Goldberg, D. and Williams, P.A. (1988) *A User's Guide to the General Health Questionnaire*, Windsor: NFER-Nelson.

Goldstein, M.J. and Miklowitz, D.J. (1994) Family intervention for persons with bipolar disorder, *New Directions for Mental Health Services*, 62: 23–36.

Goldstein, M.J., Rodnick, E.H., Evans, J.R., May, R.P.A. and Steinberg, M.R. (1978) Drug and family therapy in the aftercare of acute schizophrenics, *Archive of General Psychiatry*, 35: 1169–1177.

Haddock, G., Barrowclough, C., Tarrier, N., Moring, J., O'Brien, R., Schofield, N., Quinn, J., Palmer, S., Davies, L., Lowens, I., McGovern, J. and Lewis, S. (2003) Cognitive-behavioural therapy and motivational intervention for schizophrenia and substance misuse, *British Journal of Psychiatry*, 183: 418–426.

Haslerud, J., Thorsen, G.R.B. and Waldstrem. E. (1995) Psykisk førstehjelp ved katastrofer, ulykker og kriser, *Psykiatrisk Opplysningsfond*, 7–25.

Haugsgjerd, S. (1990) *Lidelsens Karakter i ny Psykiatri*. Oslo; Pax Forlag A/S.

Hogarty, G.E., Andreson, C.M., Reiss, D.J., Kornblith, S., Greenwald, D., Ulrich, R.F. and Carter, M. (1991) Family psychoeducation, social skills training, and maintenance chemotherapy in the aftercare treatment of schizophrenia. II. Two-year effects of a controlled study on relapse and adjustment, *Archives of General Psychiatry*, 48: 340–347.

Hogarty, G.E., Andreson, C.M., Reiss, D.J., Kornblith, S., Greenwald, D., Javna, C. and Madonia, M. (1986) Family psychoeducation, social skills training, and maintenance chemotherapy in the aftercare treatment of schizophrenia. One-year effects of a controlled study on relapse and expressed emotion, *Archives of General Psychiatry*, 43: 633–642.

Hughes, I. and Yeoman, J.A. (1995) *A S.T.E.P. Forward*, Cardiff: Shadowfax.

Hummelvoll, J.K. and Lindstrem, U.Å. (1997) *Studentlitteratur Lund*, Lund in Sweden: Multifine Offset.

Johannesen, J.O., Larsen, T.K. and Jonassen. C. (1998) Psykose hva er det?, *Psykiatrisk Opplysningsfond*.

Jordal, H. and Repål, A. (1999) *Mestring av Psykoser*, Bergen: Fagbokforlaget.

Kashner, T.M., Rader, L.E., Rodell, D.E., Beck, C.M., Rodell, L.R. and Muller, K. (1991) Family characteristics, substance abuse, and hospitalisation patterns of patients with schizophrenia, *Hospital and Community Psychiatry*, 42: 195–197.

Kavanagh, D.J. (1992) Recent developments in expressed emotion and schizophrenia, *British Journal of Psychiatry*, 160: 601–620.

Krisroffersen, K. (1998) *Parorende og Sesken i Psykisk Helsevem*, Bergen: Fagbokforlaget.

Kuipers, L., Leff, J. and Lam, D. (1992) *Family Work with Schizophrenia: A Practical Guide*, London: Gaskell.

Larsen, T.K. (1999) *First Episode of Non-Affective Psychosis*, Oslo: Universitetet I Oslo.

Larsen, T.K. and Johannesen, J.O. (1996) *Tidlig Intervensjon ved Psykose*, Stavanger: Undervisningssett. Psykiatrisk Opplysningsfond.

Lazarus, R. and Folkman. S. (1984) *Stress Appraisal and Coping*, New York: Springer.

Leff, J. (1994) Working with the families of schizophrenic patients, *British Journal of Psychiatry*, 164: 71–76.

Leff, J. and Vaughn, C. (1985) *Expressed Emotions in Families*, New York: Guilford Press.

Lehman, A.F. and Dixon, L.B. (1995) *Double Jeopardy: Chronic Mental Illness and Substance Use Disorders*, Chur, Switzerland: Harwood.

Ley, A. and Jeffrey, D. (2004) Cochrane review of treatment outcome studies and its implications for future developments, in H.L. Graham, A. Copello, M.J. Birchwood and K.T. Mueser (eds) *Substance Misuse in Psychosis: Approaches to Treatment and Service Delivery*, Chichester: Wiley.

Liberman, R.P. (1992) *Handbook of Psychiatric Rehabilitation*, Los Angeles: Allyn & Bacon.

Liberman, R.P. (1989) *Social Skills Training For Psychiatric Patients*, Los Angeles: Pergamon Press.

Lidz, T. and Fleck, S. (1985) *Schizophrenia and the Family*, 2nd edn, New York: International Universities.

Loffler, W. and Hafner, H. (1999) Ecological pattern of first admitted schizophrenics in two German cities over 25 years, *Social Science and Medicine*, 49: 93–108.

Lopez, S.R., Nelson, K.A., Snyder, K.S. and Minz, J. (1999) Attributions and affective reactions of family members and course of schizophrenia, *Journal of Abnormal Psychology*, 108: 307–314.

Mangana, A.B., Goldstein, M.J., Karno, M., Miklowitz, D.J., Jenkins, J. and Falloon, I.R.H. (1986) A brief method for asserting expressed emotion in relatives to psychiatric patients, *Psychiatry Research*, 17: 203–212.

Mari, J. and Streiner, D.L. (1997) Family intervention for those with schizophrenia, in C. Adams, J. Anderson and De Jesus J. Mari (eds) *Schizophrenia Module of the Cochrane Database of Systematic Reviews*, Cochrane Collaboration, Issue 3, Oxford: Update Software; London: BMJ.

Maslin, J. (2003) Substance misuse in psychosis: contextual issues, in H.L. Graham, A. Copello, M.J. Birchwood and K.T. Mueser (eds) *Substance Misuse in Psychosis: Approaches to Treatment and Service Delivery*, Chichester: Wiley.

McConnaughy, E.A., Prochaska, J.O. and Velicer, W.F. (1983) Stages of change in psychotherapy: measurement and sample profiles, *Psychotherapy: Theory, Research and Practice*, 20: 368–375.

McFarlane, W.R. (1983) *Family Therapy in Schizophrenia*, New York: Guilford Press.

McFarlane, W.R. (1990) Multiple family groups and the treatment of schizophrenia, in H.A. Nasrallah, *Handbook of Schizophrenia*, Amsterdam: Elsevier Science.

McFarlane, W.R. (2002) *Multifamily Groups in the Treatment of Severe Psychotic Disorders*, New York: Guilford Press.

McFarlane, W.R., Link, B., Dushay, R., Marchal, J. and Crilly, J. (1995) Psychoeducational multiple family groups: four-year relapse outcome in schizophrenia, *Family Process*, 34: 127–144.

McFarlane, W.R., Deakins, S.M., Gingerich, S.L., Dunne, E., Horen, B. and Newmark, M., *Multi-family Psychoeducational Group Treatment Manual* (unpublished).

Miller, W.R. and Rollnick, S. (1991) *Motivational Interviewing: Preparing People to Change Addictive Behaviour*, New York: Guilford Press.

Mueser, K.T. and Gingerich, S. (1994) *Alcohol and Drug Abuse, in Coping with Schizophrenia: A Guide For Families*, Oakland, CA: New Harbinger.

Mueser, K.T., Yarnold, P.R., Levinson, D.F., Singh, H., Bellack, A.S., Kee, K., Morrison, A.L. and Yaddalam, K.G. (1990) Prevalence of substance abuse in schizophrenia: demographic and clinical correlates, *Schizophrenia Bulletin*, 1016: 31–56.

Penn, D.L. and Mueser, K.T. (1996) Research update on the psychosocial treatment of schizophrenia, *American Journal of Psychiatry*, 153 (5): 607–617.

Pilling, S., Kuipers, E., Garety, P., Geddes, J., Orbach, G. and Morgan, C. (2002) Psychological treatments in schizophrenia: I. meta-analysis for family intervention, *Psychological Medicine*, 32: 763–782.

Pitschel-Waltz, G., Leucht, S., Bauml, J., Kissling, W. and Engel, R.R. (2001) The effect of family interventions on relapse and rehospitalisation in schizophrenia – a meta-analysis, *Schizophrenia Bulletin*, 27: 73–92.

Prochaska, J.O. and DiClemente, C.C. (1986) Towards a comprehensive model of change, in W.R. Miller and N. Heather (eds) *Treating Addictive Behaviours: Processes of Change*, New York: Plenum.

Radomsky, E., Haas, G., Mann, J. and Sweeney, J. (1999) Suicidal behavior in patients with schizophrenia and other psychotic disorders, *American Journal of Psychiatry*, 156 (10): 1590–1595.

Ruscher, S.-M., Wit, R. and Mazamanian, D. (1997) Psychiatric patients' attitude about medication and factors affecting noncompliance, *Psychiatric Service*, 48 (1): 82–5.

Schofield, N., Quinn, J., Haddock, G. and Barrowclough, C. (2001) Schizophrenia and substance misuse problems: a comparison between patients with and without significant carer contact, *Social Psychiatry and Psychiatric Epidemiology*, 36: 523–528.

Sciacca, K. and Hatfield, A.B. (1995) The family and the dually diagnosed patient, in A.F. Lehman and L.B. Dixon (eds) *Double Jeopardy: Chronic Mental Illness and Substance Use Disorders*, Chur, Switzerland: Harwood.

Smeby, N.A., Fagermoen, M.S., Nord, R., Hanestad, B.R. and Bjørnsborg, E. (1998) *Fra Kunst til Kolikk*, Oslo: Universitetsforlaget.

Smith, J. and Birchwood, M. (1987) Education for families with schizophrenic relatives, *British Journal of Psychiatry*, 150: 645–652.

Smith, J. and Hucker, S. (1994) Schizophrenia and substance abuse, *British Journal of Psychiatry*, 165: 13–21.

Streuben, H.J. and Carpenter, D.R. (1995) *Qualitative Research in Nursing*, New York: Lipincott.

Thorsen, G.R.B. (1995) Schizofreni, *Psykiatrisk Opplysningsfond*.

Turner, S.M. (1998) Comments on expressed emotion and the development of new treatments for substance abuse, *Behaviour Therapy*, 29: 647–654.

Ursin, H. (1984) *Stress*, Bergen; Tanum-Norli.

Vaughn, C.E. and Leff, J.P. (1976) The influence of family and social factors on the course of psychiatric illness. A comparison of schizophrenic and depressed neurotic patients, *British Journal of Psychiatry*, 129: 125–137.

Zubin, J. and Spring, B. (1977) Vulnerability – a new view of schizophrenia, *Journal of Abnormal Psychology*, 86 (2): 103–126.

Index